INTERTWINED

HUMBLE JOURNEYS
ON THE PATHWAY TO GOD

Cheryl McCausland & Laura Terry

Copyright © 2011 Cheryl McCausland & Laura Terry
All rights reserved.

ISBN: 146114471X
ISBN-13: 9781461144717
LCCN: 2011907019
CreateSpace, North Charleston, SC

We dedicate this book to our moms, with love.

ACKNOWLEDGEMENTS

We are immensely grateful for the love and support of our husbands and children. Our gratitude spills over to our dads and siblings. We recognize the experiences we write about are deeply personal and private.

Special thanks to Tracy for welcoming us into her heart and for so graciously answering our numerous questions.

And kudos to James Bahan for his wonderful work and patience in creating the beautiful design on the front of the book cover.

INTRODUCTION

I have come to the conclusion that if you live long enough to reflect on the things of your past, there comes a moment when you realize God has spoken directly to you and you truly have been touched by Him. Some refer to this as a moment of grace. To benefit from such a moment you need a willingness to expose your soul to God and a place of quiet, for it is in the quiet that we hear God speak. Indeed, we cannot hear God unless we have quieted our minds, freed our souls, and opened our hearts to Him. I did not reach this conclusion overnight. It took years of reflection, meditation and prayer, and scores of conversations with family and friends.

My name is Cheryl. I am one of three women you will learn about in the pages that follow. The other women are my friend and co-author, Laura, and her younger sister, Tracy. As a result of writing this book I can now call Tracy my friend too. The three of us believe the desire to seek God is an invisible yet indispensible element in the human genetic code. As Christians, we also believe the Holy Spirit is used to move and soothe us, and motivate us to do good things. We are not experts, mind you. We are ordinary people who have had extraordinary spiritual encounters; some with the living and others with the deceased. And while some of our experiences may be hard to believe, we hope most evoke a desire in you to stand up and say, "Me too!" If you do, then we ask you to talk to your family and friends about your experiences. You will soon learn how interconnected we are to one another.

Through our stories, we hope to help bolster your belief in God and the mysteries which surround His graces. Our experiences have proven how the longings of the soul transcend time and how true love can result in intimate reassurances after death.

Before we continue, I'd like to explain how the book cover came to be. It is the first of many stories and perfectly exemplifies the nature of the relationship Laura, Tracy and I share. It also provides insight into our belief that bits of information—we call them puzzle pieces—are sent from some intangible realm in the universe to motivate human beings toward enlightenment.

After Laura and I completed the manuscript, we contemplated changing the working title to a new, more poignant one. Laura asked Tracy to give some thought to it as well. During that time, Tracy had a dream. Actually, she had two dreams. The first one was filled with vibrant colors, something she rarely experiences. In the dream, beautiful red, orange, yellow and green ribbons floated freely in the air and became attracted to one another. The ribbons wove together from all angles and were so rich with color Tracy didn't want the dream to end. Several days passed and Tracy had another dream. In that dream a long slender finger appeared in the corner of a pure white book. The finger pointed to the title of that book, "I N T E R T W I N E D".

Tracy called Laura to share the details of the "Intertwined" dream. Laura then called me. We discussed the possibility of using "Intertwined" as the title, however, there were other prospects on our list, so we agreed to talk again later that day. In the interim, Tracy called Laura again, this time to share the details of the first dream. She apologized for not mentioning it earlier. She hadn't realized the relevance of the intertwining ribbons from the first dream until after she talked about the "Intertwined" dream.

"I think we need to read the dreams together. They may be meaningful, but I'm not sure." Tracy admitted. Like so many times in her life, Laura was awed. Since childhood Tracy has served as an unassuming messenger of divine communication. This time was no different. Laura told Tracy she would reflect on the dreams as puzzle pieces and would call her back. "I'll call Cheryl and see what she thinks."

When the phone rang and I saw it was Laura calling again I knew something must have changed. I listened intently as she excitedly relayed the details of Tracy's first dream and how she believed it related to the second one. She couldn't see me, but I was nodding my head in agreement. The details of the first dream were intriguing, but once I heard about the intertwining ribbons, it became clear a message was being relayed to us. "Intertwined, it is!" We re-titled the book, added the vibrant ribbons and blended them into butterflies—which symbolize spiritual transformation.

Tracy has had so many meaningful dreams, they must be the preferred method for divine communication with her. But such communication is not limited to dreams. Our stories reflect countless methods of communication utilized by God to reach out to us. Through these stories, we hope to bridge the gap between oft-misunderstood and unusual spiritual encounters and an unwavering belief in God.

It seems that now more than ever people seek comfort in their chosen faith and wish to nurture their relationship with God. If you share these feelings, you are surrounded by friends. No matter where you are in your spiritual journey; beginning, middle or end, or even if you are lingering on the sidelines unsure of where to begin, be open to the boundless possibilities for joy with God. We welcome you into our lives and hope you join us on the pathway that leads to Him.

IS THAT YOU, GOD?

As if on cue, Tracy woke up from a deep sleep. There she laid, eyes wide open, with her husband Dave beside her. He was peacefully asleep and oblivious to the miracle that was being performed on him at that very moment. While Tracy was accustomed to spiritual encounters, this one was different. It was unique and she knew it might not ever happen again.

It was God Himself standing over Dave. He was beautiful. He was pure. He was there for Dave alone. God was there to heal Dave.

He appeared as an ordinary sized man, yet His hand, which He placed on Dave's leg, was huge. And it was glowing like the waning embers of a warm winter fire.

Tracy remained perfectly still. She was afraid God would be angry with her for waking up. Before she could stop herself, she made eye contact with Him. He was not amused. She lowered her eyes in shame. Within seconds God was gone. She stared into the darkness for what seemed like hours, yearning for His return.

MAKING OUR WAY: WHO WE ARE AND WHY WE'RE HERE

Tracy's vision of God with Dave seems extraordinary; doesn't it? If I had heard the story years ago and prior to knowing Tracy, I would have listened politely and then gone about my business. But I now know Tracy and have experienced my own miracles, so I remain humbled by her encounter.

A few years ago Laura asked me to listen to Tracy's life story. It involves decades of encounters with the unseen. Laura also asked whether I would be willing to write about some of the things I would learn. Her motivation was to provide validation to her sister's God-given abilities and to relay a message of hope to the many individuals who struggle to incorporate similar abilities into their daily lives.

I am an attorney. I was born inquisitive and have made a living delving into the details of situations. The prospect of a provocative investigation into the interplay among psychic abilities, spirituality, and faith was irresistible. Laura wanted to show how these seemingly disparate tenets were, in fact, deeply connected, or as we write, 'intertwined'. I eagerly signed on and began to ask questions. In the process, I reflected on my own spiritual journey and awakened to the purpose it serves in my life and the lives of my family and friends.

Laura, Tracy, and I live typical American lives. We care for our families and tend to household chores. We work outside the home. We have good days and bad. We've lost people we loved and prayed for those we didn't. The three of us have something, rather, someone else in common: Annette. Actually, we don't share the same Annette but we do share the same Annette moments, and the circumstances surrounding these moments are too striking to be ignored. Upon sharing our accounts with one another we became certain these women were sent by God at points in our respective lives when our hearts were heavy and our spirits low. The encounters occurred when we were exhausted of most human emotions, the most destructive of which is fear. We now realize we had yearned for God's graces but first needed to release the fear which, like an invisible captor, locked out light and truth. No longer bound by fear, our souls became available for enlightenment.

Each 'Annette moment' resulted in the spiritual renewal, moral bolstering, and clarity within our hearts necessary to pursue our respective journeys toward God. Without fear the journey is more direct and painless. The secret is to begin and then strive always to move forward.

As pivotal as our Annette moments were, they were not singular spiritual experiences. We've had many, the most unconventional of which involve Tracy, so let's begin with her.

YOUNG TRACY'S NIGHTLY VISITORS

When you meet Tracy you are immediately struck by her calm and uncomplicated manner. She is kind and thoughtful, and her compassion toward others is immediately and perpetually apparent. Although I've never seen auras around a person, Tracy seems to emit white light. It's as though she is not weighted down by her being. She is at the same time peacefully passive and indefatigably strong. She speaks of God matter-of-factly and never dwells on the whys and why nots of it all.

Tracy is in her forties. She's been married for over twenty-five years and has three children. She is also one of five children. In her youth she struggled to be heard over the bantering of her siblings. Indeed, while she vied for attention during dinnertime conversations, it wasn't the lack of attention that bothered her; it was the lack of acceptance for who she was. You see, Tracy was different from most kids, and she certainly is different from most adults I know. Her involvement with the spiritual world, the realm of the "unseen," began at an early age; some may say too early for a child to handle. It continues to this day.

Tracy doesn't recall the first time she was visited by "people" others didn't see, but she figures it was sometime before her fifth birthday. Night after night she would awaken to the spirits of unknown individuals gathered around her bed. They always came in the middle of the night while the rest of the family slept. To her, they were quite real and their failure to speak or smile scared her more than anything else. Sometimes she gathered enough courage to run across the room she shared with older sister Laura and leap into bed with her. Once there, she would hold on to Laura until morning broke.

At first, Tracy never said a word. She didn't know how to describe the events that led to her fears. Laura simply thought her little sister struggled with weird nightmares and figured it was easiest and most comforting to let Tracy sleep with her.

Over time, Tracy shared bits and pieces of information with Laura. She talked about the people she saw and how they made her feel. She complained about how they always woke her from a deep sleep. They were expressionless and came in groups to look at her, as though she were being inspected. Some visitors had scary faces, but they were the exceptions. Usually the people seemed harmless enough; it was their bedside presence that frightened Tracy. Laura soon realized her sister's nightmares weren't typical, but being young herself, she couldn't figure out why.

Sometimes Tracy screamed out for her parents to come quickly. These experiences were the worst. Through her tears she would describe the visitors and their actions and beg her parents to tell them to go away and leave her alone. She was tired of being woken up in the middle of the night;

she just wanted to sleep. Time and again and with varying levels of compassion, patience, and concern, her parents attempted to address her claims while avoiding chaos with the rest of their children. First they would check under the beds and then inside the closets. With an "all clear" between them, they would reassure their young daughter everything would be alright.

Skeptics easily could dismiss Tracy's claims as the active imagination of a five-year-old; so could concerned parents. Indeed, they believed their daughter's nightmares were the byproduct of anxiety and fear that accompany kindergarten, and they openly hoped she would grow out of them. With the exception of Laura, Tracy's siblings ignored her stories about these visits; only Laura believed them to be real.

Laura may have had reason to believe her sister's tales. She recalls sensing an indescribable energy during her sister's encounters. When she was awakened by Tracy's fidgeting, she would lay motionless in anticipation of "something" happening. To Laura, whether or not Tracy imagined the things she talked about, her experiences were real and debilitating and kept the two of them up for hours every night. Something had to give. Before long, something did. One particular encounter altered the nature of the sisters' relationship forever.

A FOOTBALL PLAYER COMES HOME

Tracy was nearly six and Laura nearly ten. They shared a very large bedroom with another sister. They loved their room. Each girl had her own bed and there was sufficient space to play without getting hurt.

It was the middle of the night and everyone in the family was asleep. Like so many times before, Tracy woke up, startled. Normally she would wait to say anything, but this time, out of the corner of her eye, she saw a teenage boy with dark hair standing in the doorway. He was wearing a green and white football jersey and became startled when Tracy sat up in bed. Instinctively, Tracy screamed and blindly ran to Laura for protection.

"There's someone in the hallway!" she declared.

Dazed, Laura shot up out of bed. Although Tracy's nightmares were part of their nightly routine, this one was different. Tracy never screamed so frantically. Typically, Laura would inspect the doorway and hallway and then reassure her sister everything was in order. Not tonight. As Laura held her sister and prepared to step off her bed, she saw the boy. She gasped. He now stared at both of them from the bedroom doorway, but did not move. The sisters stood frozen with fear. In a split second, he turned away from the doorway, crossed the hallway and entered their brothers' bedroom. Still motionless, they watched as he swiftly moved through the boys' room and exited through the wall surrounding the bedroom window. Now they both screamed. Before they blinked, their parents sprinted up the stairs.

At the top of the upstairs hallway the girls rambled on about the football player, gesturing wildly to help make the point. In consistent detail they described him, his clothing and his actions to their mother and father. With fury, their father began an intense search. He assumed the boy was hiding somewhere inside the boys' room. He looked above, below, and through every nook and cranny. He then searched the entire house. Nothing! Nobody! He concluded a local teen must have broken in for whatever reason and ran away when Tracy woke up. Both girls protested. It didn't make sense. They watched him move through their brothers' room. Not one window was broken or opened; not one screen was torn or removed. There were no remnants of clothing or fingerprints and no shoe prints on the floors. The house was intact; nothing was out of place. Even the front and rear doors remained closed and showed no sign of forced entry.

It was late and their father was not interested in arguing with his daughters. Everyone was directed to go back to bed. The sisters obeyed, but continued to protest. They instinctively knew the football player wasn't from their neighborhood; he wasn't from *any* neighborhood! As real as he seemed, he wasn't alive; he didn't breathe! He didn't escape through the window; he faded from sight through the wall surrounding the window. They both told their father this, but at that moment he didn't want to hear it.

For Laura, Tracy's perpetual claims of visitations by the unseen were finally substantiated. She began to understand the impact such nightly encounters had on her little sister. She secretly hoped her parents would treat Tracy differently. Now that Laura also shared an encounter, the exact same encounter, Tracy's stories would be considered more plausible, right?

When morning came, nobody in the family talked about the events of the night before. Perhaps too surreal and raw to discuss, the kids had breakfast and dispersed without saying a word. Looking back on the situation, Laura now realizes her parents were probably overwhelmed and under enormous pressure to maintain a semblance of normalcy for all their children. Indeed, claims about a boy dressed as a football player dissolving into a wall must have been too fantastical to comprehend.

Time passed and the story of the boy, like so many other stories Tracy had conveyed over the years, faded away. The family moved into a new house. The sisters were a little sad because they loved their old house, especially their bedroom. Tracy asked Laura whether she thought the nightly visitations were tied to the old house. She hoped they would stop once the family moved. Her question was soon answered. Not only did the visitations not stop, they actually increased.

Tracy became consumed by her experiences and their implications. Still too young to fully comprehend what was happening, she became frightened by the prospect of never having control over her life. Her insecurities were compounded by the lack of credence given to her perpetual stories. The experiences took their toll on her emotionally, intellectually, physically and spiritually. As time went on, Tracy didn't know who she really was and what was expected of her. Her encounters were unlike anything any of her friends went through and she learned not to say much about them for fear of being ridiculed or shunned.

Upon reflection, Laura believes the football player was the first of many puzzle pieces presented to her for purposes of spiritual growth. She believes God enabled her to see the football player to affirm her sister's abilities and to open her heart to the realm of the unseen.

Interestingly, when the sisters were adults their parents matter-of-factly told them about a young man who played high school football in their home town during the 1940s. They learned he had died after a long illness. He also had lived in their old house until he passed away. The girls did not ask questions; indeed, they did not say anything at all.

GOD'S GIFTS TAKE TIME

As a high school student, Tracy began to have intense dreams in which deceased individuals shared personal information about their living loved ones. Sometimes Tracy would be asked to relay specific information to the loved ones; other times, she'd be asked to listen to the lingering issues between the living and the dead. Initially, she didn't know what to make of the dreams, but as she opened her soul to the encounters she became more of a willing participant. She made an effort to be present and engaged during the subliminal communications and even gathered the courage to relay some of the messages. Unfortunately, the recipients of the messages were not always pleased. Some even viewed Tracy's involvement as invasions of privacy. Not wanting to risk further alienation, Tracy decided to keep the messages to herself.

While this was happening, Laura was away at college. Like most college students, she spent her time studying, socializing, and preparing for future employment. Her passion was interior design, but her major was in business management. Her dad had reinforced the importance of a college degree, and from the time she was young he pushed Laura toward traditional corporate employment. She accepted this and did her best to enjoy her time at school. Wrapped up in her own life, she didn't focus much on Tracy or her other siblings, for that matter. She was aware, however, that Tracy was angry and sad, and she felt sorry for her.

Tracy failed to integrate fully into high school life. She struggled with class work and shied away from school-oriented activities. Now, every night involved a meaningful dream or visitation. The encounters drained Tracy's energy. When the morning alarm would ring, she'd awaken like a zombie and force herself to muster enough energy to get through breakfast and then the school day.

It was just a matter of time before her parents were called to meet with teachers and administrators to discuss Tracy's staring sessions and naps during class. Keenly aware of their daughter's struggles, her parents brought her to numerous doctors who ordered medical examinations and tests. After one such test, Tracy was erroneously diagnosed with epilepsy and was prescribed medicine to reduce the possibility of seizures. She knew she wasn't epileptic but trusted in her parents' sincere motivation to help. She even rationalized that taking the medicine would permit her to sleep more soundly and focus more easily.

The medicine didn't change anything, and Tracy rebelled. She hung out with the wrong people and snuck out of the house at night. She was angry and blamed the world for being forced to take medication. She felt detached and isolated. Medication was ruling her life. She felt as though she were on a merry go round—constantly moving, but not making progress. Her parents continued to downplay her accounts of nightly encounters and relied instead on the advice of medical professionals. At the time she didn't realize how much they just wanted to make things right and to help her get some badly needed sleep. Eventually, Tracy no longer wanted to be dependent upon strong prescriptions, so she weaned herself off and forged ahead.

Now a senior in high school, Tracy realized she had an innate ability to "know" facts about other people, facts about which the individuals themselves were unaware. With this new ability came new burdens. It was one thing to have conversations with the deceased in her dreams; it was another one completely to have knowledge of intimate details about the health and well-being of the living. Like before, Tracy initially shared her knowledge with some of the people, but their reactions mirrored those of the recipients of her dream-messages. It seemed that no matter how well intentioned she was, Tracy's communications often caused pain or confusion. Sadly, Tracy decided to remain silent. An example is in order.

Tracy worked as a cashier at a local grocery store. The job was convenient and comfortable since she knew most of the people who worked and shopped there. One day a woman she'd never seen before came directly up to her even though the remaining registers were free.

"Are you open?" the woman asked.

Tracy nodded, 'yes'. The woman immediately began to place grocery items on the counter. In between tallying the goods, Tracy looked at the woman and realized she was very sick with disease. She saw an unhealthy aura surrounding the woman and sensed the dark energy that seeped inside her. She didn't know whether the woman was aware of her advanced illness, so she continued to bag the groceries while she silently debated the pros and cons of sharing such sad news. Ultimately, Tracy said nothing. Instead, she called Laura to discuss the anxiety and confusion caused by knowing such personal information about other people. To this day, Tracy struggles over her decision not to say anything.

Tracy began to ponder the role of God in her life and what He had planned for her. She wanted to share information, but now would do so only with people she considered safe, like family members and close friends. Before she did, however, she would gauge the person's willingness to believe that God was working through her. Her strategy worked well most of the time, but on occasion it backfired horribly. Now fearing a total loss of friends and respect of family members, Tracy decided to distance herself from large groups and troubled individuals. Sadly, she learned to live in the shadows of conversations and to avoid drawing attention to herself.

By this time, Laura was a working member of society. She was dating her now husband Curt and having the time of her life. The benefits of earning a living, like having nice clothes and new shoes, and enjoying restful vacations, were immensely appealing. She worked hard and began to enjoy the fruits of her labor. She also became wrapped up in material things and what they represented. Success, achievement and happiness; they were one in the same. Laura's life was moving forward and she spent little energy on her younger sister's struggles.

God then sent Dave to Tracy and the pieces of her life began to fall into place.

DAVE: A DIVINE AND GLORIOUS GIFT

Dave was the dear friend of a young man who had liked Tracy for a long time. He was the double in a double date she agreed to go on, and the man she instantly knew she would marry. When Tracy first saw Dave, he was seated in the back of her date's car, alongside the girl he had asked out. She immediately noticed the warm aura surrounding him. She smiled and said hello. He smiled back. The date itself was uneventful, but before they parted ways, Tracy did something she never did before. She asked Dave for his phone number.

"Sometimes I need a ride to the mall. Could I call you?" She asked, coyly.

"Sure." Dave quickly responded to the opening. Tracy giggled as she wrote down the numbers. Within days she seemed to need a ride, called Dave, and they began to date.

Dave was a take-charge kind of guy and from the beginning was very protective of Tracy. Indeed, she felt safe in his arms. They dated for a little over a year before Dave enlisted in the Army and asked her to be his bride. With the blessing of both sets of parents, Tracy and Dave left for

Denmark to be married and then to Germany, where he was stationed. She was immensely happy.

Tracy became acutely sensitive to energies, both good and bad, and in people and places alike. She describes her sensitivities like this.

"Light energies are emitted by people and things while dark energies are absorbed. Prolonged exposure to either type exhausts me, but dark energies are especially debilitating. When I'm exposed to dark energy it's as though the air is being sucked right out of me."

To this day, Tracy must remove herself from intense energy situations before she succumbs to their effects, like severe headaches and emotional exhaustion.

To accommodate her sensitivities, Tracy looked for employment in a profession that provided flexibility and some level of cover. She chose waitressing. As a waitress she is able to socialize comfortably and avoid, or seamlessly fade from, negative energy situations.

As a newlywed, Tracy was cautious not to overwhelm Dave with the particulars of her abilities, so she shared them in bits and pieces. Before she said anything, she debated the pros and cons of sharing such details. As eager as she was to talk about them, she was afraid of his reaction to her extraordinary experiences. *Where do I begin? What should I say? How much is too much? Will he believe anything?*

Tracy started by telling Dave about her dreams. He was intrigued but treated them merely as amusing stories. But she didn't give up. Over time she fed him new and more detailed information. His reaction was consistent. He loved his wife and loved listening to her stories, but didn't treat them as recitations of actual encounters. At some point

Tracy threw caution to the wind. Secure in Dave's love, she needed him to understand that her experiences were real. She woke him up after a particularly unusual encounter. He wasn't frightened by her story because he wasn't frightened by her, but he still didn't grasp the depth of her involvement with the unseen. Something had to give. It did one evening when a soldier visited them both.

A SOLDIER'S VISIT WITH TRACY AND DAVE

When Dave was discharged from the Army, he, Tracy, and their oldest child settled in Florida, but they sorely missed New York. After a couple of years and two more children, they moved north and rented a quaint old farmhouse on the north fork of Long Island. The property on which the house was built was owned by an established farming family, and at one time had been used to grow potatoes. The owner told Tracy the farm had been in the family since the Civil War and that U.S. President William Howard Taft, a friend of a prior owner, had been a guest there.

As soon as Tracy saw the house, she knew it was haunted but didn't care. It was old and charming; it had character as well as history. Tracy easily sensed the warmth of memories lingering throughout the house and thought it to be a good place to raise a family. Before the family moved in, however, Tracy told Dave it was haunted.

Shortly after they settled in, the unseen "residents" of the house made their presence known not only to Tracy, but to her family members as well. Actually, only Tracy saw the prior residents, the others just sensed or lived the effects of their presence. They had lived in the house during the Civil War era and some had been members of the Union Army. They regularly paced around the house as though on guard for enemy infiltration. Tracy became acquainted with them as well as their individual habits and routines. Having them around became commonplace.

Of course, the residents had no awareness of day or night. When they wanted Tracy's attention, even though she was asleep, they'd come to her side of the bed and pull off her covers. She would often quietly admonish them to come back in the morning. After all, she had young children and needed her sleep. Occasionally, the residents would move over to Dave's side of the bed and tug at his covers until he woke up. He didn't find the routine amusing but knew enough not to upset them. Although his wife had shared lots of unusual stories with him, now it became personal. He figured the residents really weren't interested in him, just his wife. With Tracy's help, Dave learned how to communicate his need for sleep as well.

Most times the residents obliged, but sometimes they persisted in their efforts by waking up the kids. As young as the children were, they were able to demonstrate for their parents how the bed covers would move off of them "all by themselves" and "like magic". That's when Tracy put her foot down. She scolded the residents and accused them of acting like children themselves. They got the message and left her kids alone. Tracy never shared the specifics of the 'magic covers' with her kids. They weren't afraid and she didn't want that to change.

One evening, as her family slept, Tracy woke up, startled. She had just had a vision of Dave wearing a Confederate

A SOLDIER'S VISIT WITH TRACY AND DAVE

soldier's uniform and being carried over a trench of water by a fellow soldier. His commanding officer was looking into his eyes and telling him to stay strong. The officer was pleading with Dave not to die. Tracy was present in the vision as an emotional and concerned observer.

The vision faded. Dave awoke suddenly and sat straight up in bed. He looked around the room to get his bearings and saw his wife staring at him. Wide-eyed, he said, "I just had the strangest dream."

"I know." Tracy immediately responded having realized what had happened. She had read his dream. Dave wasn't fully awake and chuckled at his wife's assertion.

"Now, Tracy, I know you have special abilities and you can do a lot of things, but reading my mind is *not* one of them, thank goodness!" Dave was insistent in a pleading sort of way.

Tracy smirked. "You're wrong!"

"Prove it!" Dave challenged. Tracy recounted the specifics of her vision. Each detail was perfectly described. Dave shook his head in disbelief.

Tracy relayed the entire vision, moment by moment, to her husband. When she finished, her voice became hushed. She leaned over and softly explained, "You were such a young soldier; your commander couldn't bear to see you die."

Dave's eyes welled with tears. Tracy had described his dream perfectly. He was speechless. Tracy was elated. Although Dave still couldn't fully comprehend Tracy's involvement in the world of the unseen, his respect and admiration for his wife grew.

Laura looks back on this exchange between her sister and brother-in-law and cannot help but be grateful that

God indeed, had given Dave to Tracy. She also is confident God sent Curt to her. She was only fifteen at the time. They dated steadily until Christmas Day 1982, when they became engaged to marry. The wedding was scheduled for the following summer to take advantage of the warm weather. As luck would have it, their wedding vows were exchanged on Long Island in 1984 during a drenching summer rain. Despite the wet clothes and gray skies, they happily shared the day with family and friends. After the honeymoon, they settled in New Jersey and began to save for a house. Laura worked her way up the corporate ladder. She was among few women managers and although she remained unmotivated by the work itself, her salary began to mirror her status in the corporation. Like many people who were fortunate enough to earn sizeable salaries throughout the 1980s, Curt and Laura were drawn to expensive cars, nice clothes, and big houses. With each purchase, however, Laura struggled with a growing sense of emptiness.

I didn't meet Curt or Laura until 1987, when I began dating my husband, Tim. He and I were reintroduced at a law school reunion and spent hours talking about our families and friends. I was a litigator on Wall Street, and he was a financial planner for an insurance company. Although we both lived in New York City, we shared a love for the great outdoors. Tim, very much the urban sophisticate, spent his summers on the same lake upstate New York as Curt and Laura. They were among his closest friends. Actually, Curt's brother married Tim's sister, so they were family as well. From the moment I met Laura I knew she was different; she was special.

In 1989, Tim and I married near that lake in upstate New York. I had envisioned autumn's ample foliage providing colorful background for our special day. Unfortunately, our wedding took place during Hurricane Hugo. It poured all morning. My mother tried to reassure me by repeating the old adage 'rain on your wedding day is good luck.' Based on the rain that fell, we were destined to have years of it!

Tim and I continued to live in the City. At that point he worked as in-house counsel for a long-established bank, and I was a well-paid litigator. Like Laura, I justified my misery with each paycheck I cashed. It seemed the tradeoff for being well-paid was not having a life—or much of one. I worked long hours six days a week, and the routine eventually took its toll on me. I was exhausted. I wanted out of the city life and lifestyle. I wanted to breathe.

We wanted to start a family and found ourselves in need of fertility treatments. It seems the stresses of litigation took their toll on my reproductive system. The years we spent trying to get pregnant were not fun, and they were not easy. Worse, they were far from romantic. Now thirty-four and painfully aware of my biological clock, I was aggressive in my endeavors to join my friends and family members in parenthood. Tim pushed back a little. He was not as certain about the propriety or extent of our efforts. The friction between us was palpable; we spent more time together in silence than we did in conversation. I soon felt empty inside and questioned the wisdom of my desires.

EMOTIONAL TRAGEDIES CREATE EMOTIONAL VOIDS

On September 11, 1991, Tracy and Laura's mom tragically succumbed to lung cancer. She was only forty-eight. She was a beautiful woman who exuded quiet strength, like so many women of her generation. She always seemed to know what was going on, but never intruded on the privacy of her children unless the situation required it. Her insightful mannerisms helped shape the personalities of Laura, Tracy and their siblings. She was independent enough to find employment outside the house, but always put the needs of her family first.

Laura recalls an endearing nightly routine. Her dad would arrive home from work just before dinnertime and be greeted by her mother. They would have a drink together in the living room and talk about the events of the day. When they finished their drinks, the family would sit together for dinner. Laura reflects on those sweet moments for solace when she finds herself lost in the pain of her mother's death.

As their mom became weaker from disease she required many hospitalizations. Each of her children visited as often as their lives permitted. Her youngest child, a son, was only eighteen at the time.

When Tracy visited, she would be affronted by the pain and discomfort her mother endured from unrelenting medical treatments. Like the rest of the family, Tracy felt helpless and depressed. She couldn't escape the impact of physical exhaustion on her mother's being. Gone was the woman who welcomed their father home and joined him for a drink before dinner. Gone was the sweet voice of loving guidance for her children. She now appeared to be shrinking spiritually as well as physically.

One day, this proved too much for Tracy. God must have known that.

Tracy came to the hospital and greeted her mother by saying, "Mommy, I want to take away your pain." While at her mother's bedside, Tracy submitted to the invisible power of the Holy Spirit. As both women closed their eyes, Tracy placed her hands over her mother's chest. A moment later Tracy opened her eyes to witness her mother pain-free and at peace. Tracy emitted nothing but light and love in the hope of providing momentary relief. Time stood still. A few minutes later Tracy gently removed her hands. Her mother thanked her and smiled. Her smile revealed an unspoken acknowledgement of her daughter's special gifts.

Tracy thought back to a conversation they recently had shared and found the strength to accept her mother's destiny. It took place at a time when her mother was still undergoing regular and numerous chemotherapy treatments and her kids were taking turns driving back and forth to the hospital. They all chipped in. On this occasion, Tracy agreed to bring her mom to the appointment. She drove in silence since conversations often became too taxing. Before they arrived, however, her mom turned to face her and began to speak.

"It really doesn't matter what you look like on the outside Tracy; it's all about who you are on the inside. Since you were a little girl, I've known how very special you are."

"Do you remember how Dad and I would check on each of you before we went to bed?"

Tracy nodded.

"One night, when you were young, I walked into your room to wish you and your sisters goodnight. You were talking in your sleep. I walked over to hear what you were saying. You were reciting all the details of my day; where I went and who I was with. I couldn't believe my ears. You had been in school all day and had no way of knowing what I had done. When I came home from work that night I made dinner while you all did your homework. I didn't discuss my day with any of you. I was amazed."

Her mother admitted there were several more encounters just like the first one. She told Tracy how much her amazement grew each time she listened.

Various emotions swelled within Tracy. She was grateful her mom decided to share such an extraordinary secret and elated to have a deep connection with her, but she was sad. So much time had gone by since she was a little girl. So much had happened. Now her mother was too weak to linger in prolonged conversation about her special abilities and what she believed to be God's role in it all.

Tracy still wonders why she was able to disclose her abilities to her mother and why it happened during her sleep. Perhaps it was because those peaceful and intimate moments permitted her mother to be open to the possibility of spiritual intercession. Perhaps it was in those moments that her mother took refuge in the soul of her gifted child and felt no pressure to succumb to social norms.

The untimely death of a parent can leave a child feeling empty and lost, creating a void that no one, no thing, and no amount of time can fill. Such is the situation with these sisters. Their mother's passing caused a sense of longing and emotional restlessness with which they continue to struggle. Their grief, like that of their siblings, was raw. At the time, no one in the family could fully comprehend the impact of the loss. Each was wrapped in pain, unable to seek or provide comfort. Laura described her family's mourning as being separate silos of emotion. She laments not having had the spiritual and emotional maturity to have reached out to her younger brothers and sisters, or for that matter, her dad.

Now mature adults, the sisters reflect on the impact of their mother's death on their dad. When she died they were numb to their father's pain. They now realize he was required to remain strong for his family while adjusting to life without his wife. Such events form the nuances of our journeys.

Laura is now about the same age as her mother was when she died. She wonders how her mom felt spiritually once she knew her life was coming to an end. Learning her mother's perspective on life and death would have enabled her to peek into her mother's soul. To this day, Laura regrets not having engaged in deep, insightful conversations with her mom before it was too late. To be sure, she always told her mother she loved her, but never was able to convey her appreciation in tangible detail. She wanted to confess how her mother's very essence—the manner in which she spoke and acted and the life lessons which she taught—permeated Laura's life. Her failure to share these most intimate thoughts resulted in a painful yearning and a void that has magnified rather than diminished over time.

A little over a year after her mother died, Laura gave birth to her first child, Morgan. She spent most of her pregnancy wondering what her mother would have thought, or said, or done, to help her along. As immensely happy as she was, becoming a mother herself only intensified the sense of loss. But she focused her love on Morgan and through prayer, sought guidance from her mother.

Laura took full advantage of her company's maternity leave but eventually had to return to work. She and Curt resisted having to place Morgan in daycare, but there were bills to pay. They had grown to rely on both incomes to maintain their homes and lifestyles. Laura juggled the obligations of work, family, and household, and the desire to have another child grew stronger with each passing month. But her routine didn't exist without consequences. In heartbreaking sequence, she became pregnant then miscarried time after time. With each loss she grieved more deeply. She began to view her work obligations as increasingly intrusive and no longer believed her career was central to her happiness. Her perspective on things was changing, but she didn't realize to what extent.

When Morgan was four, Laura became pregnant again. Fearful of another miscarriage, she was acutely sensitive to every ache, pain, and bout of nausea that filled the first trimester. As the pregnancy progressed, she became completely in tune with the life growing within her and prayed to God for a healthy, full-term baby. Her prayers were answered, and they were blessed with another healthy baby girl, Carsen. This time Laura's sense of protectiveness and responsibility was heightened. She wanted to stay home with the girls, no longer motivated by work in an industry void of meaning. She and Curt reconfigured their financial obligations, and Laura took extended maternity leave.

Now home all day with baby Carsen, Laura was eager to provide a warm and loving environment and decided to decorate the nursery. She spent time in the room to envision furniture placement and wall hangings. She knew what colors she would use on the walls, but couldn't quite decide where to place the crib. If she placed it by the window the natural light would bathe Carsen in warmth and provide natural distraction. If she kept Carsen closer to the doorway, she wouldn't be exposed to winter's chill.

One afternoon, as Laura paced the room, different sections became cold and drafty. She found it odd, especially since the heat was on and the windows were closed. The curtains framing the windows began to sway as though a strong summer wind were blowing. Laura looked around for an obvious cause. Finding none, she continued with her efforts. At that moment Morgan, then five, walked into the nursery. She had been downstairs quietly playing with her toys in the family room, and climbed the stairs in near silence. Laura turned to see Morgan by her side. She bent down to remind Morgan to speak quietly but was interrupted. Morgan matter-of-factly told Laura that "grandma" was in the room with them and wanted her to tell her mom to keep the furniture the way she last had it. Then Morgan giggled.

"Grandma said not to move it anymore." Not wanting to wake the baby, Laura now kneeled and leaned into Morgan to make sure she had heard correctly.

"Who, honey?" she asked.

Morgan responded, "Your mother, Grandma." She then walked downstairs and returned to her toys.

Laura was stunned by Morgan's message as well as her demeanor. She spoke so matter-of-factly! Laura wondered whether Morgan had had previous conversations with her mother. She knew to carefully tailor her inquiries to avoid frightening her daughter and soon learned that Morgan had been visited by many people who had passed on and not just her grandmother. Some of them were nice, but others were not. Laura felt a queasy sense of déjà-vu.

UPWARDS AND ONWARDS: TIM AND CHERYL SWITCH GEARS

Tim and I spent years unsuccessfully trying to get pregnant; change was now in order. We agreed to leave our jobs, begin the process of adoption, and open a "mom and pop" law practice upstate. Before we moved, I surprised him with one last vacation. We ate and drank and had a great time and returned energized for our new venture.

The day after I gave notice to my employer, I learned I was pregnant. Not only was I pregnant, but I was carrying twins. During the initial sonogram, Tim turned pale white. He didn't move or say much. As I wiped the sweat from his brow and reassured him everything would work out fine, I prayed to God that my optimism was warranted. At the age of thirty-four I was carrying twins. Wow! In the blink of an eye, Tim and I became unemployed expectant parents preparing to relocate to a rural town without the benefit of a client base. Now that's freedom!

We moved into a small old house on the edge of town and opened the business with pressured anticipation. Months later we were blessed with two healthy boys and joined the legions of parents woken up in the middle of every night by the cries of their hungry young. I felt like a cow, nothing short of a milking machine! Tim worked long hours while I tended to the twins. We barely slept and rarely spoke for more than minutes at a time; we lacked the energy to do so.

When Connor and Duncan were almost seven months old I became pregnant again, this time without medical involvement. The news completely overwhelmed me. I cried to my mother, and confessed my anxiety over the level of care and love I would be required to give.

"God doesn't give us anything He knows we can't handle. You and Tim will love this child as much as you do the twins. You will have plenty of love to give and you both will be blessed with a child that steals your hearts. Don't worry; trust me."

I relied on her words of wisdom. After all, with six kids of her own, she knew what she was saying.

When I was five months pregnant, we moved into a beautiful new house that was located next to a famous fly-fishing river. The pregnancy was relatively uneventful until three weeks before my due date. It was January 1996 and after weeks of bone-chilling temperatures and record snowfalls, a heat wave overtook the area. In the course of one afternoon, the four feet of snow that lined the banks of the river melted. As it did, the river outside our back door began to rise. First tree branches, then picnic tables and benches, floated past our back window. Before long there were boats and mobile homes.

By late afternoon I called Tim to come home. The roof was leaking and puddles dotted our living room floor. He did his best to fix the roof, but the rain wouldn't let up.

UPWARDS AND ONWARDS:

The boys began to splash around, their laughter providing minimal but necessary comic relief. Shortly after dinner I realized I was in pre-term labor. I tried not to panic, but my obstetrician was more than sixty miles away. By early evening our community was in a declared state of emergency, and we were forbidden to travel on the highways.

The main road by our house was blocked on one side by falling ice from a bridge over the highway and on the other by an overflowing river. We had no way to get to town. Family members began to call. My doctor tried to coordinate the landing of a helicopter on the closed state highway, but the weather was too treacherous and the state police denied his request. We were isolated and desperate, a mere two miles from civilization.

There was another complication. Our ninety-two year old neighbor, Bea, lived alone and refused to leave her house. Bea was what you call "old stock"—tough, stubborn, and immune to outside pressure. When we asked her to stay with us, she dismissed our plea with furrowed brow.

"If God intended me to go this way, then, by golly, I'm going," she confidently proclaimed.

That was that; there was no more conversation. By nine o'clock the river was so swollen I called 911 to learn our options for rescue. Seemingly unmoved by my pathetic ramblings about the kids and Bea and the baby, the operator robotically admonished unless we wanted a rescue boat sent out immediately, I was to hang up because other needy individuals were trying to get through to her.

Did she say a boat? Rescue by boat?

Tim called the doctor and was instructed on how to deliver a baby. Now he panicked. The only way to minimize having to deliver the baby himself was to calm me down and make me rest. I immediately promised to do my part, indeed, anything, to avoid giving birth in the house in front of our toddlers.

The river continued to swell. Tim diligently monitored its proximity to the house.

"We'll leave when the river gets to ... the top of the steps down to the river ... the maple tree in the backyard ... the fence in front of the back deck ... the outer edge of the back deck ... the inner edge of the back deck ... the inside of the door to the back deck."

The last thing I recall before falling into a deep sleep was Tim telling the doctor everything was going to be okay.

Shortly before dawn the river crested and then slowly began to recede. By the time the boys woke up, my labor pains subsided sufficiently for us to venture outside and check on Bea. She was fine, as she assured us she would be. Our community, on the other hand, was devastated. Many people lost their property, several even lost their lives. I was emotionally drained, and poor Tim was exhausted. My doctor suggested I have the baby the following day, three weeks before my due date. I agreed. After all the commotion, our daughter Lily was born, the boys were safe, and all was well in our world.

When Lily was a few weeks old, my parents invited us to come to Florida. Tim wasn't able to leave the office, but thought it best if the rest of us got some sun. I was excited. As soon as the plane landed in Tampa I removed our coats and sweaters and noticed how pale we all looked. I couldn't wait to take Lily for a stroll in the park and let the boys play at the beach with my folks! Unfortunately, none of those things came to pass. Three days after we arrived, Lily contracted an upper respiratory virus and was hospitalized. She wasn't even a month old. While she was in the hospital both boys were stricken with a horrendous stomach virus and were unable to eat or drink.

Connor became severely dehydrated. So dire were his circumstances the local pediatrician urged me not to wait for an ambulance, but to drive him to the hospital myself. Dazed and exhausted, I drove with one eye on the road and the other on my rapidly deteriorating son. Nearly lifeless in his car seat and unable to move, I gently reassured him how much he was loved and that "everything was going to be alright." Two hospital staff members were waiting for us at the emergency room entrance. They quickly took him from me and began their efforts to save him.

Connor was placed in a different hospital ward than Lily. My parents cared for Duncan while I spent the next twelve days traveling to and from the hospital. I felt sorry for myself, but not for long. Lily was located in the back of a pediatric oncology ward. Each time I visited Lily, I first had to pass by young children stricken with cancer. It was heartwrenching. The routine became too much to handle. One morning I went to the hospital lounge, sat myself down and began to cry. The stress was killing me and I felt as though I had the weight of the world on my shoulders. A doctor saw me crying and after listening to my tale of woe, gently but firmly put things into perspective. He pointed to the parents of the children being treated on the oncology ward.

"The difference between you and them is that you know your kids will leave this hospital. They don't." It was the sobering truth. I felt ashamed.

With lots of help and prayers, my kids healed. We were cleared to leave for home. When I met Tim at the airport, I fell into his arms. As we hugged, I realized something had changed in me. I had matured as a mother. I was scarred but keenly aware of the blessings God bestowed on Tim and me. Our children were healthy and had just gotten sick; they were not children whose very existence teetered from day to day.

ANNETTE, THE FIRST TIME

In what was later learned to be a big fat test of Laura's will, upon her return from maternity leave, she was assigned to a management training program in Atlanta. It was an intricately planned week of grueling work and intense stress in steamy hot summer weather. Laura had returned to work with a very heavy heart and was extremely unhappy about the prospect of being away from her family. Perhaps it was too soon to be so far from her infant daughter; perhaps she realized that no amount of money could take the place of the joy she felt while caring for her girls.

The program required teams of employees to build mock race cars. The winning team would share a significant bonus. The stakes were high and the competition was fierce. Laura was determined to integrate herself back into the company, but from the moment she arrived, she felt things weren't quite right. She was emotionally and psychologically removed from her colleagues, like an outsider looking in. She shrugged off the initial sense of isolation and focused her energy on the effort to get her team to the finish line. She knew her team could win and she was determined to do just that.

Day one of the competition began with a simulated visit to the Department of Motor Vehicles, complete with ornery, obstinate employees. The DMV office was set up outside of a main tent which acted as a "garage" to house the contestants and their cars during the competition. After satisfying DMV personnel, Laura obtained the necessary permits and entered the garage to lead her group. As the day went on, she learned how members of other teams had plotted to steal auto parts to keep their competitive edge. She became extremely concerned over the tone of the competition, but was determined nonetheless to win.

The heat was unbearable; the humidity, intense. The garage that housed the competitors failed to protect them from the heat. Laura felt queasy and light headed. She soon became disoriented and felt out of sorts. A colleague noticed and encouraged her to take a break.

"I don't know what it is, but I feel extremely odd right now," Laura admitted. She made her way into the hotel and slowly headed toward her room. As she did, the hallways began to close in on her and she felt as though she were in a maze. She knew she had to get into her room as quickly as possible. When she opened the door, a colleague named Annette was sitting on one of the beds. Laura was both surprised and relieved; she liked Annette very much. Annette was a bright, diligent, manager's assistant who was also kind and approachable. Her southern charm and calm demeanor blended perfectly with her wit. Laura knew she would be a great roommate.

After a quick hello, Laura said apologetically, "Something's wrong with me. I don't feel right." Annette smiled sympathetically and had Laura lay down. In an effort to reassure Laura, she talked about being assigned to lead her own team and how unhappy it made her. She admitted to feeling a bit overwhelmed herself. Now calm, Laura highlighted Annette's numerous management skills and how she was able to handle any challenge. Instead of being appreciative, Annette snapped back at her.

"No, you don't get it! You can just work your way through a competition like this, even if you don't feel comfortable. That's just the way you are. You will do whatever you have to to get the job done. I can't. I'm not like you."

Laura was startled. Annette had just repeated what seemed to be the story of her life. Laura always did what was expected of her. She always took intense ownership of her projects and completed every task—even at great personal expense. Suddenly, those traits seemed wrong and misguided. Annette's directed observation cut through Laura and left her feeling slightly ashamed. It was as though she looked at herself in the mirror and saw the warped reflection of another person.

At that moment Laura felt herself being pulled into an emotional space she didn't know existed. It was inner chaos; her entire being was turned upside down. Struggling to hold on to a waning sense of reality, an overwhelming energy took hold. She became passive. While powerless, she remained fully aware of her surroundings. Conscious of every word she was saying, time slowed down. Laura then turned to Annette with an unyielding need to repent.

Words of regret began to tumble out of her mouth. She spoke about the choices she had made in life, and how she was not proud of some. She reflected on her many decisions and how they may not have been the right ones. She also spoke about relationships—who was important to her and why. She knew she didn't want to be away from her family any more; she knew they were more important than any project or competition. She couldn't stop herself and didn't want to either.

Over and over Laura asked Annette, "Am I in heaven? Am I in hell? Are you my guardian angel? Are you my mother?" There were many things about Annette that reminded Laura of her deceased mother, especially her mannerisms. Desperate to understand what was happening, Laura clung to her last question.

And then it happened. Laura's voice dropped to an octave far deeper than she had ever heard; its cadence and intonation was foreign to her. The voice was not her own and she could not control it. Words poured out of her as she purged the sense of evil that had dwelt within her. All the while, Annette sat directly across from her, engaged and calm. And then it stopped. Vulnerable, Laura looked at Annette for reassurance. Her reaction was not what Laura expected it to be.

Laura asked Annette if she had heard the change in her voice. Annette smiled and knowingly nodded her head in agreement. Before Laura passed out from exhaustion, she wondered, *Am I a demon? Shouldn't Annette be frightened? Was this experience only meant for me?*

Later that evening, Laura awoke to silence and darkness. Annette was asleep in the next bed. Looking around the room in an effort to determine whether she had dreamt the entire exchange, Laura's eyes were drawn to the ceiling. There were plastic stars above her. She then glanced over at the bedside table to see what time it was. Next to the clock was a plastic rainbow. *What the heck is going on?* Laura wondered. *Are these real? Did someone place these things in my room? Did they just appear?* Still too exhausted to figure it all out, she rolled over and went back to sleep.

The next morning Laura walked over to the window with heightened senses and looked outside. It was beautiful; the flowers and trees were vibrant and colorful. Like Dorothy in Oz, the greens had never been so green, the blues, never so blue. She was filled with joy as she listened to chirping birds. She paused to linger in the simplicity and beauty of it all, having never before experienced such pureness of being. With unique and newfound appreciation, she thanked God, realizing his role in her life-altering encounter.

Annette woke up. Laura turned her attention away from the window and back inside.

"What happened to me?" she asked pleadingly.

Annette reminded Laura she came to the room to rest because she didn't feel well. Then she said something unexpected.

"It's okay, Laura; it was necessary. Everything happened that was intended," Annette reassured.

Necessary? What an unusual way to describe what she had just been through. What did Annette mean by that? What exactly did she witness and what was her role in Laura's life? Laura chose to reflect on Annette's explanation before she responded.

Both women had to prepare for the day and reviewed the planned schedule of events. As they spoke, Laura knew her life had changed; she had been born again. She was lost in her own thoughts when her manager called. He said he wanted to bring her to the hospital, as a precaution; he wanted to be sure she wasn't ill. Laura agreed to go, secretly struggling to hold on to the familiar instead of succumbing to the peace that was growing within her.

After a thorough check up, Laura was given a clean bill of health. She was not dehydrated, ill, or suffering from post-partum depression. Although the term "nervous breakdown" wasn't mentioned, the possibility certainly lingered in Laura's thoughts. The experience she had the night before was either a nervous breakdown or a spiritual cleansing. Either way, she expelled the emotional and spiritual darkness that had contained her for years, and in the process, she scraped the grime off her soul. It was her spiritual awakening.

Before returning to the competition, Laura called Curt. Worried about his wife and recognizing the uneasiness in her voice, he offered to fly to Atlanta and bring her home. She promised to call him later in the day, but within hours Laura knew she needed to go home to her family. When Laura told Annette, she smiled and announced she would escort her back to Newark.

On their way to the airport, Laura realized she had been a "perfect storm" of spiritual, physical, and emotional conflict—a cataclysmic psychological event just waiting to happen. She thought about being home with her husband and her girls. The rat race was over. The two women didn't speak much on the flight home, but as the plane prepared to land, Annette prepared Laura for the surge of emotions she would have when she saw her family. She was right. Laura was a mess. She was tired of juggling the responsibilities of family, work, and home.

"Let's go home," Curt said as he put his arms around her. "You'll be okay."

"Are you sure?" she asked him.

"Yep," he whispered.

Laura looked at Annette with gratitude. She knew Annette had been sent to guide her through her spiritual cleansing. Now saying goodbye, there was nothing Laura could say or do that Annette didn't already know. They shared goodbyes. Before turning away, Laura asked Annette if there was anything she could do for her. Annette just smiled and asked Laura to send "refrigerator art" from her girls. The women chuckled and embraced once more. Annette turned away from the family and prepared to board the next plane back to Atlanta. Laura never saw Annette again.

Laura was humbled by the experience, but with a lingering need to insert logic into the situation, she asked Curt whether he thought she had suffered a nervous breakdown.

"I don't know," he admitted.

Curt didn't push Laura to talk about what had happened, but did keep a keen eye on her. If what she felt in her heart was real, she had been reoriented by the Holy Spirit to be the mother and wife she had always wanted to be. Her spiritual journey was propelled forward. Each day, with the blessing of her husband, she sought opportunities to have the Holy Spirit guide her. She was astounded by the multitude of moments and experiences that affirmed her newfound path. Her heightened awareness and appreciation for this 'second chance' permeated her every thought.

One such experience came a few weeks after Laura stopped working. She had an incredibly vivid dream that a dragon-like being lived inside of her. It had no wings or feet, but had a tail. It had lived inside her for a long time.

Toward the end of the dream, the dragon-being squirmed and struggled in its efforts to be released from her body. It spewed fire as it came through her mouth and then flew free. Laura woke up. She recognized that the dream was important, but didn't know why. She needed time to decipher its meaning.

Months went by. Laura began to practice yoga. She spoke with a male friend who, like her, had once been driven by success in his career and now lived a more balanced life. They openly acknowledged the significant emotional changes that occurred once they eschewed their old ways. They spoke about the practice of yoga and how it enabled a sense of control and calm that had been missing in their lives. The conversation made Laura reflect on her routine. Each morning she would set her mat down on her living room floor so that it faced a favorite piece of artwork. The artwork was a gift from Curt and contained a circle, a spiral, and soft, wavy lines. She didn't know why she sat in the same place all the time other than it was comfortable and somehow comforting. Now intrigued by her routine, she investigated the symbolism of the shapes to determine whether there was a reason she was drawn to them.

Laura learned that spirals are ancient symbols of the womb, fertility, feminine strength, change and evolution of the universe. Circles universally symbolize unity, wholeness, and infinity. They sometimes symbolize the power of the feminine and the sun. Laura recalled the dragon-being from her dream and decided to research dragon symbolism in literature. Depicted in almost all cultural writings since ancient times, fire-breathing dragons symbolize leadership, passion, vitality, and mastery. So why was the dragon in her dream desperate to escape her body? After much reflection, Laura deduced the dragon dream was a continuation of the cleansing process begun in Atlanta; a necessary step to expel the darkness that had lingered inside her. She believes the dragon's escape represented her rebirth.

In *Why is God Laughing*, Deepak Chopra writes, "Whatever captivates you is also trying to wake you up."[1] Laura's love for her daughters captivated her and led to the extraordinary decision to leave her employment. Her quest for spiritual knowledge also captivated her and woke her up to the many possibilities for communication with God.

Information designed to enlighten Laura endlessly streamed to her without regard to day or night, and it came by way of signs, symbols and dreams. When Laura shared this with me, we likened the messages to life preservers cast to lift human beings from spiritual darkness and ignorance. Indeed, we both believe information is provided from outside the realm of consciousness for the express purpose of being combined with human intuition. The goal is spiritual growth. Each bit is a puzzle piece which, if construed properly, creates a unique pattern designed for enlightenment.

Consider it this way: haven't you been in situations where you've thought *that's strange*, *what a coincidence* or *I wonder what that means?* Rather than invest the time to construe the meaning and import of the encounter, many of us eschew the information, release it from our consciousness and throw it back into the universe. What a waste! Imagine if we collectively reoriented our thought processes to actively seek information, reflect deeply on its meaning, and then discuss our contemplations with one another.

Distractions such as computers, televisions, movies, and cell phones would be replaced with quiet meditation and thoughtful conversation and with it a resurgence of spiritual enlightenment and prophetic vision. We are designed for this enlightenment, but have gotten too distracted. God is everywhere and available to us anytime, therefore we must seek and embrace Him in quiet reflection.

SEPTEMBER 10, 2001: IS THAT YOU, MOM?

Tracy and Dave spent the day undertaking the many chores required to maintain an old farmhouse. They were exhausted and wanted to go to bed. Despite the late hour, the evening air remained hot and sticky. Their bedroom was located on the first floor of the house and opened into a parlor. Inside the parlor was a huge picture window overlooking the backyard. Earlier, Dave placed fans strategically throughout the house to circulate the air as best he could. This included the one located in the doorway to their bedroom. The system wasn't perfect, but it provided enough of a breeze to enable them to sleep.

Within minutes of getting into bed, the fans began to sputter slowly, as though about to short out, and then ease back to rhythmic usefulness. Tracy was certain the "residents" were behind the electrical shenanigans but was too tired to explore communications. The dysfunction of the fan in their doorway particularly distracted Tracy. She became upset and got out of bed to resolve the interruptions. As she headed toward the fan, she was distracted by movement coming from the parlor. She initially feared an intruder was outside peering into the house through the window.

She peeked into the parlor and out the window. It was her mother, motionless and staring in at her. Frightened, she fell backwards towards the bed. Determined to confirm what she saw, she lifted herself up and walked toward the doorway again. Again, she peeked out the window from behind the doorway; her mother was still there. Her face was beautiful but expressionless. She was devoid of the warm aura she emitted during previous visitations.

Their eyes met. Her mom seemed startled and upset at being seen. Tracy became emotional. So did her mother. Tracy stood frozen in the doorway and didn't know what to do. She finally gathered the courage to call out, "Mom?" and then fumbled for a light switch in a confused effort to see her better. Her mother disappeared as soon as the light went on. The fan in the doorway eased into motion and remained on for the rest of the night. Tracy didn't sleep. Of all the spirit encounters with her mother, this one troubled her most.

Later that same night Laura was also visited by her mom. She didn't actually see her like Tracy, but was given a message by her nonetheless.

Laura spent the day thinking about her mom. The next day marked the tenth anniversary of her death. Prior to going to sleep, Laura closed her eyes to pray and visualized every detail of her mother's beautiful face, lustrous hair, toned body, and kind mannerisms. Sadly, as the years passed, this became harder to do. She wondered what her mom would look like if she were alive now and what their relationship would be like. At thirty-nine, Laura longed to look her mom in the eye and have deep conversations about things like motherhood and marriage, and she longed to be silly with her too. Immersed in prayer, Laura spoke aloud as though her mom were kneeling next to her beside the bed. Before a final "amen" Laura asked whether her mom was watching over her and her family. Emotional and frustrated, Laura fell asleep.

In the early hours of the morning Laura woke up from a deep sleep. The room was pitch black. She rolled over in bed to look at the alarm clock on her nightstand. As the numbers came into focus, she became startled by something moving directly above and in front of her. There was a beautiful, luminous, cross floating in mid-air. She was mesmerized by its presence. As the cross dissipated into the dark room, Laura became immensely grateful for her mother's reassurance that she was at peace with God and was, indeed, watching over her.

It was the morning of September 11, 2001.

Weeks later Laura and Tracy pieced together the timing of their mother's visits with the infamous terrorist attacks and wondered whether her spirit was aware of the impending human tragedies. They'll never know.

THE ENERGY SHIFT OF 9/11

All situations present opportunities to learn about ourselves and bring us closer to God. The tragic events of 9/11 fostered renewed interest in the responsibility we have to one another. The terrorist attacks amounted to a wake-up call to the human race; the boundaries which once separated us from one another had shrunk. In the process it condensed mankind's collective awareness into pointed reality. It seems Americans especially realize they are no longer removed or protected from the rest of the world.

Our behavior affects the behavior of others, no matter how far away; it also impacts the behavior of those who come after us. As a result, there must be a consolidated effort to right the teetering moral ship of humanity and nurture our souls in a manner worthy of God's graces.

In Christianity, Christ is the church, and each Christian is one in being with Christ and the church. Metaphorically speaking, each person is an integral part of the body of Christ. Therefore, whatever harm we do to another, we do to ourselves; destructive acts against another are actually self-inflicted acts of violence. The events of 9/11 spotlighted the crossroads at which we find ourselves, spiritually speaking. Do we move ahead collectively toward God, or do we splinter away from the rest of the body? The hatred that motivated the violence ironically led to a renewed call to love and be loved, to tolerate and to be tolerated. The "silver lining" in this evil event could be humanity's unwavering defense of life, all life, and tolerance toward our differences.

Relationships are what we have been given here on earth. Community and communication are essential to our spiritual existence and growth. God has given us one another for the very purpose of sharing our "selves"; our ability to love is the essential divine gift that separates us from other living things. It is our responsibility to promote a sense of community with this gift and to actively participate in each of our relationships to do so. We must always be conscious of love and open our hearts to the grace that permits it to prevail.

Our relationship with God should be protected and nourished above all others. We should never engage in behavior that is contrary to love. This requires us to think before we act. I reflect on my own behavior throughout life. I sometimes envision slips of paper containing detailed descriptions of my actions being scrutinized by angels who are charged with determining whether to place them into a box stamped *approved* on judgment day. Just the thought of that possibility makes me shudder. As a work in progress, I am grateful for each opportunity I get to improve my chances of making it into that box!

WHISPERINGS

Curt is a good man. Laura learned this on her first date with him. She also had the good fortune of learning early in the relationship that they would marry. It was summer and they were on a date. It was a gorgeous afternoon at the lake, so they spent it riding around in Curt's boat. When the date was over, Curt drove to Laura's house and began to dock the boat. Laura stayed seated. A soft voice whispered into Laura's right ear, "He's the one."

Laura instinctively turned toward the voice, thinking it was Curt, but no one was there. She turned her head around once more just to make sure. Curt secured the ropes and helped her onto the dock. While she didn't dwell on the event, the voice in her ear provided insight into her life's journey.

Laura was comfortable enough with Curt to discuss matters of the spiritual and unseen, including her experiences with Tracy. Like Dave with Tracy, Curt listened intently and was fascinated, yet he had never had such experiences and failed to fully comprehend their importance. Indeed, Curt became somewhat numb to the intrigue surrounding Laura and other family members. Stories of spiritual messages, visitations and dream interpretations seemed to roll off his back. That changed one evening when, years after she died, Laura's mother visited Curt.

It was Saturday and Curt and Laura were dressing for an important business dinner. With the finishing touches nearly complete, Laura walked over to the jewelry box located on her dresser. Next to it was a small vase that had a plate-like base. In there she kept a pair of diamond studs. They were a special gift from Curt and had immense sentimental value. Although Laura didn't have occasion to wear them often, she regularly checked the base of the vase to make sure they were there. In fact, earlier that day she peeked to silently confirm how they'd complement her outfit. Now ready to complete her look, she gently reached into the base with two fingers to pick up the first stud, but the base was empty. Confused, she lifted the vase, then the base, and then scoured the entire area, including the bedroom floor. The earrings were gone! Laura panicked. Did she unwittingly place the earrings inside the jewelry box? She didn't.

Who was in the house? The girls were, but they hadn't been in the bedroom. Some repair men also were, but they worked downstairs only. Laura initially dismissed the possibility that it could have been a workman, but with no other conclusion to draw, she told Curt. As a precaution, he contacted the police as well as their homeowners' insurance company. Laura was very heavy-hearted. The police thoroughly searched the house for evidence of theft and finding none, cleared the repair men of any possibility of wrongdoing.

Laura knew there was more to the missing earrings than met the eye, but she couldn't quite put her finger on it. In the days that followed she spent hours thinking through various scenarios to explain their disappearance. The earrings were missing for a reason; she just needed to figure out why. Curt tried to get her to accept reality but she wouldn't let things go.

Two weeks passed, and it was Saturday once again. The girls relaxed in the family room while Laura folded laundry in the bedroom. It was late afternoon. Curt had worked in the yard all day and came in to shower. He walked upstairs to let Laura know he was finished. She thanked him and began to talk about the earrings again, but he was tired and dirty and just wanted to shower. He listened for a moment and then closed the bathroom door behind him.

Laura returned to folding the clothes. She remained quite bothered by the situation, partly because of the sentiment, partly because the disappearance made no sense. Minutes later the bathroom door slammed open. The banging startled Laura. Curt stood in the doorway, dripping wet, with a towel wrapped around his waist. He was visibly shaken. Laura ran over to him.

"What is it? What's wrong?" She asked, thinking he didn't feel well. Dumbfounded, he blurted out, "Someone came to me while I was in the shower. I heard a voice. It might have been your mother. She told me the earrings were back now."

They rushed over to the dresser and sure enough the diamond studs shined brightly from the base of the vase.

"Someone came to me; spoke to me; and told me the earrings were back." Curt held onto Laura. He was simultaneously perplexed, relieved and amazed. Laura was ecstatic over her mother's visit. She laughed and gave him an enthusiastic hug. Her mother's involvement may have explained the disappearance, but why she did it remained a mystery.

"Do you think she needed them for a fancy party up in heaven?" Laura asked. They both laughed.

Since then Curt has experienced many "knowings", where instructions are "whispered" to him to find missing items.

Over the years, Curt's willingness to open his heart to the involvement of the unseen in life events deepened his respect for Laura, their kids, and her family. Laura knows God is responsible for these encounters yet remains perpetually aware of the complications they create. Tracy's childhood pain and confusion are not distant memories; they are a constant in Laura's consciousness.

It is a mystery as to whether Laura's family hit a spiritual jackpot of sorts, one that includes generations of gifted individuals predisposed towards communication with the unseen. Both of her daughters have abilities that appear to fall within the same realm as Tracy's, but to what extent she remains uncertain. I wonder whether heritage plays a part in spiritual sensitivities.

TRACY IS MOST ACTIVE WHEN SHE SLEEPS

Inside dreams Tracy feels safe and relaxed, even when the dreams themselves are not so pleasant. She knows that dreams, themselves, are not harmful, even though the messages relayed may cause pain. She also knows that spirit guides use dreams to communicate important information to those who are unreceptive to it during waking hours. She explains:

"Spirits communicate with me during dreams. They often appear in human likeness and as far as I can tell, they are very much present. They look directly at me, but almost never speak in a traditional sense. They communicate through symbols. They read my mind and then share information with me. I've often held beautiful conversations without any words being spoken. I have intimate conversations with spirits; it's as though we are sitting together in the same room."

Tracy points to one such dream involving her mother-in-law. Dave's mom had passed away several weeks before the dream and the family missed her terribly. In the dream Tracy's mother-in-law sat in a favorite lounge chair. She looked beautiful, happy, and at peace. Tracy communicated how much she missed her and how beautiful she looked. In response, her mother-in-law assured all was well, but she advised that Dave needed to get a box to hold his many recipes. Tracy agreed with her, and they both laughed. She told Tracy she loved her and then slipped away.

Tracy was captivated by the dream. Earlier in the day Dave spent hours looking all over the house for his mom's famous Christmas cookie recipe. They were a family favorite, and he wanted to bake them for his dad in memory of his mom. No matter where he looked, he couldn't find the recipe card. When Tracy told Dave about the dream, he chuckled and admitted to being a bit jealous that his mom picked Tracy to visit and not him. He agreed to do what she asked and left to purchase a recipe box for his recipes. When he returned home, he found the recipe card. Would he have located the card on his own and without his mother's admonishments? Does it matter? The dream provided happiness and direction to Tracy and Dave. Isn't that what matters?

Some of Tracy's dreams have implications far beyond her family. She has had dreams about famous people and tragic events, the details of which have caused her extreme anxiety over whether she should "do something" or "tell someone" the information. One such dream involved the space shuttle Columbia the night before it tragically blew apart. In the dream, Tracy saw a huge eyeball, similar to the one located on the United States dollar bill. The eye was looking down from the heavens onto the launching pad for the space shuttle. As the eye observed from above, the shuttle engines thundered to life and the machine slowly lifted towards the sky, and the eye. There was a sudden and intense burst of flames and the dream abruptly ended. The dream was so unsettling that Tracy planned to call Laura to talk about it when she returned from work the next day. News of the horrific explosion broke before she had the opportunity to do so. She was frantic. In a panic, she called her sister and stammered out the details of her dream the night before.

Was the eye in the dream the Eye of Providence, or the all-seeing eye of God? Was her dream a premonition? If it was, what could or should she possibly have done with the information? Tracy's anxiety was based on her inability to know the importance of a particular dream when she has it. It is only when a situation unfolds publicly that she ascertains the importance of the dream. She doesn't know whether, when, or how to relay information to people who may be impacted by the event either. For these reasons, Tracy confides in Laura alone. Another dream more pointedly highlights her dilemma.

This dream involved the world renowned pop singer Michael Jackson. In the dream, he was on stage surrounded by dancers, singing the song "Thriller."[2] Tracy was a member of the audience. As he performed, he looked into her eyes as though he were singing to her alone. When he finished the song he disappeared.

Tracy woke up slightly confused. *That was weird. Why did I dream about Michael Jackson and what was that song he sang to me?* Never a real fan of Michael Jackson's music, she wanted to investigate why the dream unfolded the way it did and whether the words he sang relayed meaningful information. She certainly knew who Michael Jackson was, but keeping abreast of celebrity comings and goings was not part of her daily routine. At breakfast she asked her teenage daughter to help her find the lyrics on the computer. Her daughter rolled her eyes. Like so many teens, she couldn't believe her mother asked about something so obvious.

"Okay Mom, let's find the lyrics." With a few strokes at the keyboard, "Thriller" was playing on the computer. Tracy listened intently.

"That's it! That's it!" she exclaimed.

Her daughter responded somewhat sarcastically, "It's called 'Thriller' mom. It's not only the name of the song; it's the title of one of the most successful albums ever."

"Oh," Tracy replied blandly. Later in the day, as mother and daughter watched TV, the program was interrupted to report the death of Michael Jackson. Bewildered, Tracy's youngster turned and asked, "Mom, didn't you just have a dream about him last night?"

"Yes. Yes, I did." was all Tracy could say. Once again she was left to ponder why she had the dream when she did and what, if anything, she was supposed to do with it. The lyrics to "Thriller" certainly have macabre undertones, but were they sung to her as a premonition of Mr. Jackson's death?

While Tracy is incredibly gifted, she doesn't believe she is special. She believes the world is bursting with individuals who have similar abilities but remain trapped inside the fear of exposure and ridicule. Imagine what we all could accomplish if fear no longer held us hostage!

It is not folly to envision a collective and positive energy shift. History is replete with examples of seemingly impossible feats accomplished due to fearless determination and extraordinary will. As for Tracy's intriguing dreams, they are not unlike those that have piqued human curiosities throughout the ages.

We think of Tracy's dreams as being more akin to information download. 'Things' come to her through her subconscious and become available for dissemination. For this, she humbly praises God and describes herself as a mere conduit of truth communication. However, these occurrences take a toll on her, physically. After she shares truths, she is often exhausted or even debilitated. But Tracy is not alone in her spiritual journey. God has given her Jimmy. She refers to him as her spirit guide. He's been with her for years and most often appears in visions and dreams as a man in his mid-twenties with brown, slicked back hair, wearing a white tee-shirt and black boots. His purpose is to comfort and strengthen Tracy when fear creeps too closely. Years ago Tracy had what she refers to as her "Jimmy" dream. Captivating and elusive, its meaning remained hidden through the numerous life events that led Tracy to discern and implement its message.

In the dream, Jimmy approached Tracy with his arms outstretched and his hands up and opened wide. Neither walking nor flying, he appeared to come from thin air and lingered about her, just above the floor.

"You need to take a ride with me; we need to see somebody. Don't be afraid; you know I am always with you."

He took hold of her hand and lifted her off the ground. A moment later, they were soaring above the earth. She held on tight, fearful she would fall. When she gathered the courage to look down she saw huge expanses of varying time periods as though they were three dimensional landscapes. The earth itself appeared as a condensed history of mankind arranged on an interactive foundation. They slowed to a glide. The scenes below came into focus. Women in beautiful petticoats were walking on dirt streets. Horse and buggy-style carriages carried villagers from place to place. They were everywhere. It was a scene from the late 1800s.

Jimmy wouldn't linger. He led her through snapshots of life events as though they were points of interest on a cross-continental flight. Moments later they hovered above scenes from the early 1900s. Without discussing it, Tracy knew Jimmy wanted her to look at the faces of the people as they passed. She did, although she didn't recognize anyone in particular. While they observed, proud men drove past them in Model T Fords. They were snappily dressed in business attire. On the sidewalks silhouetted women dressed in period clothing made their way from building to building. After a moment or two, Jimmy led Tracy to modern day. Cars were everywhere, and they were loud. Office buildings and skyscrapers replaced quaint town squares and village greens. The scene was chaotic and distressing. Tracy didn't like being there. When she looked over at Jimmy, he turned his head to acknowledge her. With her eyes she communicated her desire to know where he was taking her and why he had her pass through various historical eras to get there. He ignored her and turned his attention to the scenes below, determined to find whatever it was he was looking for.

Within a moment or two, Jimmy recognized the scene before him. He effortlessly guided the two of them down to earth. Tracy had no idea where they were. Nobody was around. She had no way of knowing which period they were in either. While she wasn't scared, she wasn't quite comfortable with the situation.

Unfazed by Tracy's emotional state, Jimmy turned to speak to her like a parent whose child was about to board the school bus on the first day of kindergarten. He prepared her for some of the things she was about to encounter. She had an appointment with an individual he described as knowing what was best for her. He was emphatic: "Tracy you need to open your heart and to listen to Him. He has something very important to tell you." Not knowing what else to say, Tracy agreed to do her best. Jimmy then pointed her to a door and left her to contemplate what was to happen next.

Tracy slowly walked toward the door. When she reached it, she knocked gently then entered a darkly paneled room. Barely able to see, she noticed the outline of a person seated in a large chair. Daring not to move, she gazed around the room and sensed she was inside a judge's chambers. As her eyes adjusted to the dim light, Tracy saw a man seated behind a beautiful wood desk, and assumed he was the person Jimmy wanted her to meet. As her eyes fully adjusted, the man, wearing powdered wig and judicial robe, looked directly at her. She surmised she was in England during the nineteenth century. Concerned about why she was standing before a judge, Tracy opened her eyes wide, but dared not to speak.

The judge looked up from his desk and warmly gazed through Tracy, inspecting her from the inside out. A moment later his expression turned serious as he focused his eyes on hers. Calling her by name he said, "Tracy, you need to be a stronger person; you need to go back to the other side and be a stronger person." While she wasn't afraid of the judge she remained keenly aware of her obligation to listen and obey. He then faded away and her dream abruptly ended.

Tracy woke up and immediately documented the dream. Clearly the judge was either God or an angel and the message was intended for her specifically since she was called by name. She wondered what to do with the directive to "be a stronger person" and knew to let the dream incubate in her thoughts for awhile.

ENTRANCE ONTO GOD'S PATHWAY SOMETIMES BEGINS ON A SIDE ROAD

When my family returned from Florida, I agreed to work part-time to help with the bills. The increasingly stressful schedule caused me to lose all indications of my prior self and the life I had in New York City. I knew Tim had become disenchanted with the practice of law and tried my best to accommodate his dreams alongside the needs of our children. Within a year or two, Tim no longer wanted to own a small-town law firm; he wanted to do "something else." He lost focus. I became angry. Time passed. We barely made ends meet. At Tim's urging, I took a job as a municipal attorney.

My responsibilities often led me to work late then drive like a lunatic to the kids' daycare center before it closed for the day. As soon as we'd get home it was mealtime, bath time, bed time; there simply was no *me* time. Lost in the rigors of my family's schedule, I didn't sing, laugh, or pray. I wasn't fully engaged in any faction of my life; this was especially so when it came to the kids. While I kept the household together and running smoothly, I did so with a numb sense of love.

Things changed one Friday night in January 2003. I had become accustomed to cold, snowy winters, but they took their toll on me. That winter was no exception. The temperature had hovered in the low double digits for weeks, and while the highway itself was cleared of significant snowfall, the side roads were pocked with black ice. Knowing this, I traveled slowly and cautiously. After work I picked up a pizza and headed home. The several-mile trip took me past the main village and onto a service road. When I turned to enter the highway everything went wrong.

The front tires of my car skid across a shelf of black ice, and the car began to slide. Despite traveling at about fifteen miles an hour and knowing not to over-correct or slam on the brakes, I over-corrected and slammed on the brakes in a desperate effort to stop the car. Reality slowed as I observed my car, with me in it, slide across the highway shoulder. From inside, I watched as the car ascended up and then over a snow covered guard rail, before descending into a short ravine. With my seatbelt tightly secured, I rotated, with the car, top to bottom, until we came to rest, upside down, in the center of a frozen pond.

In the seconds before I lost consciousness, I was captivated with the scene before me. The car's headlights were like spotlights enabling me to watch every moment of my slow motion dive into and then through the frosting-like snow that covered the pond. It was pure white and wrapped the car in brilliance. Everything was bright yet serene. It was so quiet I could hear my watch tick. Strangely, I felt at peace. As I let go of the steering wheel, I surrendered.

"Okay, God. It's up to You; whatever You want to happen, I'll accept."

I was calmly prepared to die, if that was what God intended. I passed out. When I regained consciousness I heard the sound of people banging on the driver side window. I thought I was dreaming.

"Are you okay in there? Are there any children in the car? Are you alone?"

Because I was upside down, the weight of my body on the seatbelt prevented me from freeing myself. I looked up, but couldn't see anything.

I shouted back, "There are no children in the car."

The booster seats I kept in the back of the car were now resting on the roof. With a bang and a shatter, the rear passenger window was removed and a good Samaritan unlocked the front door. Another spoke to me about what was happening and then held onto me as he released my seat belt. I was in shock and had no idea what the commotion was all about. Unaware of the scene around me, I just wanted to go home.

"If you'd just help me up, I'd like to call my husband."

My rescuers begged me to wait for an ambulance, but I dismissed their pleas. They held onto me as we walked slowly up the ravine. When I reached the top of the embankment, I saw police cars and ambulances everywhere. I panicked.

"Did I hurt someone?" I asked.

A trooper shook his head and looked at me sympathetically.

"Just yourself. You need to go to the hospital." I thanked him, but repeated my desire to go home. I borrowed his phone and called Tim. Within a few minutes Tim arrived, kids in tow, and was immediately overwhelmed by the number of emergency vehicles. Then he saw my car, upside down in the center of the pond. He thought I was dead.

I quickly thanked the trooper, ignored his request that I be checked out, and limped over to my family. The ride home was slow and silent.

We tucked the kids into bed before I recounted the details of the accident to Tim. He sat in silence and then blurted out, "I'm sorry. I know I'm staring at you; it's just that I'm expecting your arms to fall off or for you to drop dead."

I took some Tylenol and we called it a night.

The next morning I read an article in our local paper about a man who, like me, skid off the road and into a pond. Unlike me, however, his car broke through the ice and he drowned. I was nauseous. Why him and not me? Why was I allowed to live? God had been with me in the car, right by my side; wasn't He also with the man? I recalled my last moment of consciousness the night before when I entrusted my destiny to Him and calmly accepted the prospect of death.

Weeks later I learned about the driver who had stopped for gas alongside the highway when I swerved on the ice. As he filled his tank, he looked into the dark cold night at the moment my car careened over the guard rail. He saw the headlights of my car travel up into the clear winter sky, then down into the frozen abyss. He called out for help and then called 911.

I regularly return to the moment when I "let go and let God" and meditate on my response to the emerging crisis. My faith has been strengthened not because I lived, but because I was given the opportunity to trust in God, and did just that. My pivotal conversation with God oriented me onto the pathway toward Him.

NOURISHMENT ALONG THE WAY: READING FROM THE GOOD BOOK

In June 2005, some person yet to be found intentionally set fire to the government office where I work. The fire caused Lily, then nine, to fear my life was in danger. It triggered her memory of the 2001 terrorist attacks on the Twin Towers in New York City. Two days before the attacks, my family was in lower Manhattan and I shared stories about the years I worked on the fifty-fifth floor of Tower Two. The kids were fascinated. Two days later the Towers were gone. After the fire in 2005, Lily became obsessed with the notion that someone was trying to kill me. Our attempts to reassure her failed, so Tim and I recalculated our finances, and I resigned.

After being home a little over a week, I began to read the Bible. The year before, I volunteered to teach sixth grade at Sunday school and was intrigued by the stories of the Old Testament, but nothing prepared me for the amazing journey on which I embarked. As I read the passages, I purposefully reflected on the words and their meanings and soon became lost in another era, place, and dimension.

I vacillated between feeling blessed and completely unworthy; yearning to be with God but not wanting to die just yet. It took me one year to read the book, cover to cover.

I came to view death as a graduation of sorts, a moment of complete change. It is the pivotal transition from the physical to the spiritual. As a Christian I believe in eternal life and to me, death is the beginning of forever. I meditated on events such as birthdays. Once a person dies his birth date is no longer relevant. A birth date can be likened to a date of conception. Conception is important only so long as a child is unborn; once born, the date of conception is meaningless. So it is with birthdays and death. Once a person passes over to the other side of life, the day on which the person was born is really no longer relevant. The renowned psychologist Carl Jung theorized there is a psychic existence beyond time and space. He believed that death should be our goal; it is part of the process of working through humanity, in an inclusive way, to reach the recognition of divinity within. I like his theory.

In the year that transpired, Lily forgot the traumatic events that caused her fears. I returned to work part-time, but was a very different person than when I left. God first, family next, the rest of the world, get in line. People noticed. Grateful for my inner transformation, I was comforted knowing, spiritually speaking, no one could hurt me.

REINFORCEMENT: A VISIT FROM MY GUARDIAN ANGEL

The nuances of my journey have made me more receptive to God's messages. Some come by way of car accidents and inspirational words, others through visions and dreams. This particular night I was not asleep, so I was not dreaming. It was three thirty in the morning. Suffering from insomnia, I initially planned to get out of bed, but then simply remained next to my sleeping husband to await the six o'clock alarm. My attention was drawn to the bedroom doorway. An invisible but very real presence entered the room, best described as a solid mist. I was captivated and unafraid. The presence glided slowly above the bedroom floor before stopping at my side of the bed. It was the height and width of a human adult but had no physical substance. As I lay there, I was overtaken by a gentle electric sensation before being embraced by the ethereal being. It then melted into my skin, and the tingling sensation inside my body faded. As quickly as the presence appeared, it was gone.

I turned to Tim and waited for him to say something, but he didn't. I went into each of the kids' rooms to make sure they all were in bed. They were. I returned to our room and woke Tim.

"Tim, Tim, did you just hear anything?"

He mumbled a sleepy, "No."

"Did any of the kids just come in?" I asked.

"Huh? No." He rolled over and went back to sleep. I stayed awake for the remainder of the night and tried to comprehend what had happened to me. In the morning I asked Tim again whether he or the kids had gotten up; he said they had not. There was no logical explanation for what I saw and felt, and yet it happened and I know it involved God. Was it my guardian angel? Was it the Holy Spirit? Why did I allow myself to be swept into its heavenly hold? Was I now supposed to do something?

Numerous publications acknowledge the phenomenon of intense spiritual activity in the middle of the night. Tracy believes spiritual beings trapped between heaven and earth seek out contact with human beings when we are at rest. I now believe my guardian angel was sent to reinforce my faith and to prepare me for the next encounter with God.

ANGELS EXIST EVERY WHERE: ANNETTE, THE SECOND TIME

My life was jammed packed with obligations. Work, teaching, marriage, children, and household chores left me incapable of personal reflection. I was a walking void. My relationship with Tim was strained and I was emotionally and spiritually fragile. I had become obsessed with our financial security to the detriment of my emotional attachment to him. While I brought home a steady paycheck, he explored entrepreneurial dreamscapes. It never dawned on me that my husband was seeking his own epiphany.

The situation took its toll on us, and, we soon learned, our kids. One night, after a particularly emotional argument, our kids left a children's book on our bed with a note tucked inside. They wrote how much they loved us both and how sorry they were, for what I did not know. When I realized what we had done to them, I wanted to vomit. I cried for them. I cried for myself. I also cried for Tim. We tried our best to explain that they were not responsible for our issues, but, like most kids, they just hung their heads in shame. It was my lowest moment as a parent. I still have the note, and I still cry when I read it.

The pressure in my chest was daunting and constant. I avoided extended contact with people and quickly excused myself from conversations and social gatherings. I knew I needed emotional release, what I didn't know is that I needed emotional cleansing. I soon received both.

It was a holy day of obligation for Catholics. I went to Mass during my lunch hour. I felt safe in church. While there, sadness rose up through me like water from a well. I kept my head hung low and prayed for guidance and peace. As soon as Mass ended, I swiftly exited to make my way back to the office. On the sidewalk in front of me was a woman I knew named Annette. She was walking toward the church. Annette worked in a local office and was kind, intelligent, and forthcoming. She also was deeply religious and emotionally grounded.

As we approached one another, I smiled and said hello. She looked at me knowingly, and tilted her head forward.

"How are you doing?" she asked.

I couldn't answer her; the words wouldn't come out. I stood frozen before her for just a minute before I was overcome by an uncontrollable motivation to purge the fear that smothered me. The pain in my heart ruptured. I began to hyperventilate and began to speak gibberish. Annette stood still, watching guard. I heaved and cried, and then whimpered. She took hold of me. I spewed forth every ounce of pain and anger that had been locked inside of me for years. She tightened her protective embrace. I finally caught my breath.

"Bow your head and let's pray," Annette declared.

I was no longer aware of my surroundings; I was emotionally and spiritually removed from them.

Annette began: "Dear Lord, take this pain away from Cheryl; allow her to see her life and all of its goodness. Let her have the peace that she needs to take care of her family. Guide her through this situation and keep her out of harm's way. Amen."

"Amen," I whispered.

In an instant the pain and the pressure were gone from my chest, never to return. Annette was not finished with me, though. She instructed me to *stop* interfering with my husband's journey and reminded me of my obligation to God first and then to my children. She told me to let Tim go, to let him be free to explore his own spiritual journey and relationship with God; I was living a lie, and I was being deceptive to my children. I needed to trust God and to stop trying to fit His will into my ill-conceived plans.

Then she stopped. We hugged one another and I thanked her. Our separate journeys toward God collided that afternoon, and we now share a spiritual bond that has no boundaries. God sent Annette to impart the grace I so desperately needed. He worked through her to cleanse my soul and communicate His admonishments. As I walked away I felt free. Something changed inside of me; I was emotionally clean and spiritually renewed.

This moment of grace enabled me to address my family situation with enlightened perspective. Tim was still searching for meaningful, gainful employment, we still had bills to pay, and our children still needed to be loved, housed, clothed and fed; but the pressure in my chest was gone; so was my fear. I had been blessed in the name of the Lord, and nothing could destroy me.

According to Carl Jung each human being has a specific nature and a calling that is uniquely his own, and unless a person fulfills his calling in the manner in which he is "wired," he ultimately becomes sick. I think I became sick and Annette was sent to help me heal.

After our encounter, Annette and I saw each another on occasion, but I shied away from conversation. I was afraid to talk about it. It was ironic since she was the person who enabled me to break through my fears in the first place. My concern was definitely ego-based; she could have forgotten our moment of grace together and thought I was crazy.

A couple of years later I told Laura about my experience with Annette; that's when she shared her story about her Annette. Laura realized she too had been sick and her Annette was sent to help her heal.

Through many conversations with Laura I gained the confidence to call my Annette to express the depth of my gratitude. When she answered the phone, I blurted out how grateful I was that she saved my life. She immediately knew what I was talking about. We both became emotional. She thanked God for bestowing grace on both of us and took no credit for herself. Clearly, she accomplished the task with which she was charged by God and had moved forward on her own journey.

A TIME TO LEARN

Laura felt liberated. She awoke each day feeling renewed and excited about the future. She knew her place was at home. Deepak Chopra writes, "You think it would take heroic efforts to solve the problems that face us. Spiritually speaking, the reverse is true. The soul's vision isn't about struggle and lack of results. It isn't about failure." He also writes, "You only need to measure your actions against three simple conditions: You act without effort. You feel joy in what you do. Your actions bring results."[3] Laura began to act without effort, feel joy in what she did, and enjoy the results of her new approach to life.

Since Atlanta, Laura has witnessed God's grace in motion on many occasions. Admittedly, not one has mirrored the "whop you upside the head" cleansing with Annette, but they have occurred just the same. For example, once Laura decided not to go back to work, she became more involved in her church and its activities, and volunteered to teach Sunday school. In preparation for the class, Laura was given a teaching manual. The first lesson was about Christmas. It discussed the journey of the three kings to the place where baby Jesus was born. They followed the star of Bethlehem, and it led them straight to God. As Laura read the story she made the connection between her vision of stars on the ceiling of her Atlanta hotel room and her own journey toward God. The largest star was a puzzle piece given to Laura for spiritual direction; she just needed the opportunity to decipher its purpose.

The financial realities posed by one income took their toll on Curt and Laura. After all, her earnings had been a significant portion of the family's income. Before long, they were required to make some tough choices. Laura now viewed their house as little more than a status symbol, and it was no longer meaningful.

Contrary to the feelings Laura had about her house, she loved the summer cabin the family owned on the lake upstate and the memories the lake held for her and Curt. They met and fell in love at the lake, and the cabin was a piece of the very fabric that made them a couple. It represented the essence of love to them. They knew they couldn't keep the cabin and the house; they had to choose. They kept the cabin, sold their house, and moved to a smaller one in the same community. In the process, Laura was freed from the priorities she once embraced.

When they sold their house, Laura's older daughter Morgan, then twelve, was diagnosed with panic anxiety disorder. Laura worked tirelessly with the school psychologist and a child psychiatrist to enable her daughter to navigate through the debilitating anxiety. Through it all she prayed for patience and guidance. Her prayers were answered as she witnessed her daughter's release of the hold fear and anxiety once had on her and her emergence as a healthy teenage girl.

Laura recognized how important it was for her to be at home during this especially difficult period in her daughter's life. She imagined what life would have been like had she gone back to work. She thanked God for His blessings, which enabled her to stand side-by-side with her daughter. Morgan learned as much as she could about panic anxiety disorder in an effort to manage the issues it created in her life. In the process, Laura discovered many things about her daughter as well as herself. In turn, Morgan got to know her mother. And while Laura could not comprehend everything her daughter experienced, she was immensely proud of her determination and tenacity to conquer her fears. Now older, Morgan reflects on the true blessing of having wonderful resources in her life and openly shares her gratitude:

"No words can truly express how grateful I am. Through the process I have learned to not only manage my anxiety but also to embrace who I am and appreciate and nurture the things that make me me."

As a result of becoming more involved at church, Laura recently hosted a weekend retreat at the family's newly renovated lake house. She invited her pastor and a dozen female church members to come for a weekend of prayer, reflection and conversation. Laura expected the women who accepted her invitation to be in the "same place" as her, spiritually speaking. She had never participated in a religious retreat before and was looking forward to the event with hopeful anticipation of enlightenment and renewal of spirit.

Laura reflected on her use of the term the "same place." *Do I hope they all believe in heaven? Are they all similarly positioned within the pathway to God? Is there some thing or place located between earth and heaven? And what is heaven anyway?*

With these contemplations, Laura prepared for the weekend. Her personal goal was to achieve a deeper sense of spirituality with each prayer session. She hoped to emerge with amazing revelations about God and insight into the meaning of her life here on earth. Committed to fostering conversations that enabled revelation, she began one session by discussing her experience in Atlanta. As she shared the preliminary details, she noticed some discomfort among the participants. She abridged the story and calmly waited for some life-altering feedback. Unfortunately, no one responded. Disappointed and embarrassed, she quickly curtailed the story. As the weekend progressed, Laura noticed the participants' reactions to the various prayer sessions and discussions. She was genuinely impressed with their knowledge of Bible text, and wondered whether she should focus more on the written word and less on the spiritual message.

The weekend retreat came to an end, and Laura felt empty inside. She was dissatisfied and saddened by the lack of discussion of spiritual awakenings like hers. Indeed, the conversations never led to personal examples of God's graces such as the one she experienced with Annette. She erroneously thought by being among people who seemed more 'religious', she'd attain more spiritual fulfillment. But the opposite occurred, and it bothered her deeply. What exactly let her down? Was it God? Her pastor? Was it the women, individually and collectively? Or did Laura let herself down? After all, even though no one responded to her story about Annette, she didn't have to stop talking about it. She could have pursued other discussions about spirituality and revealed even more about her own life journey. But she didn't. Why? Fear!

Laura questioned whether she was a "spiritual snob" who over-anticipated the impact of hosting such an event. The weekend clearly was meaningful to the other participants, so what was her problem? Her problem involved her ego. She equated each participant with herself and projected onto each her own exaggerated expectations. But because each person's journey is her own, God designs results meaningful to her alone, without regard to others. Each woman came to the retreat with her own soul and her own life's journey, so logically the impact of the retreat would be unique to her. Laura's lack of fulfillment was irrelevant. She was on her own journey within the pathway to God; looking to others to fulfill her own needs was foolish. It was a waste of precious opportunity to work through her ego and illuminate the common denominator among the group: God.

It is an error to view our time on earth as a race to get to heaven and foolish to compare ourselves "spiritually" to another. Who are we to judge the spiritual weight afforded a particular deed, either good or bad? We cannot know the soul of another; only God knows the soul. Only God knows the sincerity with which each of us tries. The comparisons we make to others as being "better" or "worse" in the eyes of God is arrogant and an utter waste of time.

TIME TO DELVE
INTO OUR SOULS

God reaches out to each of us in as many ways as the days are long. Through the power of the Holy Spirit, our souls can sing out to Him. As we embrace the spiritual we loosen the grip fear holds on the physical. It's that simple. Once we acknowledge life as being only partially physical, we interact in the world in a timeless and limitless manner. Upon acceptance of spiritual reality, the boundaries between the here-and-now and the life-ever-after disappear. The world of God encompasses it all. We view life as a platform for spiritual metamorphosis and believe we should endeavor to emerge from our physical shells prepared to embrace the perpetual glory of God.

If the human soul exists at the moment of conception, its development must depend on the life led by the person to whom it belongs. The uncertainty of the soul's journey emanates from the God-given gift of free will. Free will subjects the soul to human discretion, good and bad, therefore its journey towards God cannot be guaranteed. While a soul may not be able to further develop in a particular lifetime, surely it is designed to do so. Indeed, souls must be gathered somewhere in the universe, awaiting God's final call. While they wait, isn't it possible that they undertake God's work here on earth? Based on our own experiences, Laura, Tracy and I refer to this gathering as a "river of souls" available to any person who seeks spiritual nourishment.

Dark energies like fear, hatred and pain must be toxic to the soul and impede its ability to move forward. Because of this, our yearning for the light of truth must be strong enough to break through any darkness. Imagine a world in which everyone fostered the soul's evolution toward God. Imagine if we nurtured each soul as though it were a member of the greatest sports team of all time! For the team to compete, survive, and then dominate, each member must be fully healthy and strong, right? The member must be nourished and pampered and then challenged and rewarded. This analysis applies to our souls as moral warriors. With each successful spiritual evolution of the soul, the team evolves to the level of strength and endurance necessary to forge ahead and conquer darkness and fear. The team, so to speak, is the collective soul, and it is likewise evolving. With the shedding of our physical skin, our souls join others in their perpetual journey toward God. We each have a responsibility to maintain the strength and purity of that river.

The predisposition of our souls toward God continually propels us into situations and relationships beneficial to their development. That is, we must subconsciously seek out similarly situated souls in an effort to comfort and be comforted, to learn and to teach, and to renew and become renewed. Think about it. A meaningful relationship develops when thoughts and opinions are shared in a manner that fosters increased interest in another. As it does, the perspective of each participant morphs ever-so-slightly. The once separate but now merged points of reference then carry forward into new relationships, and so on. If our souls communicate with one another through relationships, then those we foster must fulfill a purpose of which we may remain unaware. All the while, the souls labor in perpetual evolution toward God.

No matter how able the soul, sometimes it needs help to connect with another. This is where the science of attraction plays a part. Attraction is the method by which one soul calls out to another; and it isn't limited to the physical, either. Surely you have found yourself attracted to the intellect, perspective, or humor of another. Think about it. The attraction causes you to want to be around that other person. While the connection isn't always meaningful or productive, it must serve a purpose. Perhaps certain relationships occur to demonstrate the boundaries within which our souls must operate. Negative or harmful relationships often prove to be important lessons about behavior to avoid in the future. With heightened awareness of the role our souls play, we can strive to benefit from each relationship and to answer the call of another's soul to find comfort and guidance.

Angels must be God-given reinforcements for our souls. They truly undertake some of the heaviest lifting here on earth. Indestructibly strong and fierce in determination, they work tirelessly to free our souls from physical bonds. When you open your heart to the existence of angels, you soon discover their intimate involvement in your life. Not only can they relay divine messages through dreams and visions but they can appear in human likeness and use whatever means possible to connect our souls to God. Laura and I view our Annettes as angels who, through the power of the Holy Spirit, emerged from the realm of the unseen to help save our souls from life's destructive tendencies. Their acts of love lifted us away from the power of darkness and fear and freed us to openly undertake God's work. Every act of good is an act of God. Since joy germinates in acts of love, true joy is the divine by-product of love. We continually seek opportunities to "pay forward" the good deeds of our angels with the goal of creating true joy for others.

TRACY EMBRACES HER JOURNEY: "ANNETTE" NUMBER THREE

Not too long ago, Tracy and Laura spoke about a cable program titled *The Children of the Paranormal*. The show presents mysteries involving teens who are portrayed as having abilities similar to Tracy's and spotlights the role of spirit beings in solving the mysteries. While the situations appear sensationalized for purposes of entertainment, the message seems valid: invisible energies surround us. The program they watched did not report the phenomena from a religious perspective yet Tracy found comfort in the media's recognition of the unseen in daily existence.

While the sisters spoke, Tracy had a revelation.

"Maybe God wants to use me as a vehicle to help people. I need to leave my heart and mind open to His words and just let Him guide me and to stop hiding. I can do that now." The message from her "Jimmy dream" finally took hold. The puzzle piece given to her years before required life experience before its purpose could be harvested. Tracy felt renewed once again and prepared to embrace the rest of her life with confidence and spiritual energy.

Maybe Tracy's spiritual journey is not meant to contain one cataclysmic event that shakes her to the core, like Laura's or mine; maybe hers is a slow and deliberate awakening that provides perpetual spiritual renewal. Perhaps hers has been more constant because her soul is farther along on its journey than ours. Tracy may well have a more developed soul. That would certainly explain many of the things she has encountered throughout her life. Perhaps because Tracy's soul is so developed she has no need to expend energy trying to figure out why she has the abilities she does; she accepts that she does, and that's that. My soul must not be as far along since I spend a good portion of my day trying to figure out the whys of my encounters and experiences. Laura seems to fall somewhere in between. She knows she "knows" things, but continues to spend time trying to figure out why. Her journey has led her to reflect on things such as the nuances of seemingly inconsequential events, whispers, intuitions, and the importance of individuals who seem to appear from thin air.

While we believe Tracy's abilities are God-given gifts, sometimes these gifts were too much for her to handle. Now a mature adult, Tracy understands her role more clearly than she did earlier in her life. She is a messenger of information and must continue to relay it with confidence that God uses her to do so. In the past many of her messages caused pain. She now sees that the pain stemmed from fear. To help others break through the fear that kept them from being enlightened, Tracy knows she must encounter and conquer her own fears. The process may not be easy, but she believes it to be necessary. A recent encounter proves the point.

TRACY EMBRACES HER JOURNEY

Tracy attended a fun-filled party to honor a neighbor of hers on Long Island. In the crowd was an old friend to whom she had given unsolicited health-related information years before. The message was not well received and caused a rift between the two. When she saw her friend, Tracy immediately reached out to offer an initial apology and then an explanation for her behavior. Her apology was not accepted. The person walked away abruptly and dismissed her attempt at meaningful conversation. Tracy was shocked and thought she may have frightened her friend. She was hurt and once again questioned whether she had misunderstood God's involvement in her life and His desires for her.

Unbeknownst to Tracy there was an angel in her midst, and her name was Ann. She was a friend of the host. Tracy did not know Ann; they had never met. The women had been on opposite sides of the front lawn for most of the party. Within moments of Tracy's unsuccessful apology, Ann came over and introduced herself. She told Tracy she thought they should talk. They walked away from the crowd of partygoers and over to a private section of the lawn. Without prompting, Ann began by explaining that she did not know what she was doing; she was not in control of her actions or her words. She became emotional and slowly receded into herself. As she did, she told Tracy she believed she was being used as a channel and that someone was attempting to communicate to Tracy through her. Tracy was intrigued.

For the next several minutes, Ann chanted various verses from the Bible. In between the verses she chanted, "God is love; you are light and love." As Ann spoke, the din of the party faded and the two women focused only on one another. Tracy listened intently to the words Ann used, eager to decipher some hidden meaning. When Ann stopped speaking, Tracy paused to comprehend what she had heard.

Ann was humbled by what had transpired between the two. While she was a spiritual person, the encounter was unlike anything she had experienced before, and the phrases she used were not ones with which she was familiar. She took no credit for the message of encouragement and politely excused herself.

Tracy watched as Ann walked away. She must have been an angel sent to affirm God's desires for Tracy, and to clear up any lingering confusion about her special abilities.

FACING FEAR

Recently, Laura gathered the courage to speak with her dad about the young football player who caused such a commotion decades ago. She wanted to know what her father really thought about the situation. She also wanted to know why he dismissed his daughters' claims. But Laura didn't want to alienate her dad; rather, she wanted to understand him. Interestingly, she never asked him to reconcile the events of that evening with the news her parents shared years later about the high school football player who lived and died in their house years before they moved in.

Her father repeated his belief that a teenager had broken into the house and that he did his best to protect his family. As he spoke, questions welled up in Laura, like why didn't he call the police. How could their parents have dismissed identical descriptions of the boy and his actions, including his exit through her brothers' bedroom wall and not the window? Laura knew her parents always sought rational explanations for Tracy's encounters, but the football player was different. Perhaps stifling fear prevented her parents from delving into the realm of the unseen to explain away the mystery of that evening. Perhaps the situation was not sufficiently dire for them to push through the fear that concealed the truth.

Fear is everywhere. It has the ability to infiltrate every aspect of our lives. It is fierce but can be overcome. When Laura and I had our Annette moments, we were devoid of control over ourselves and our ability to analyze our emotions, especially fear. Thinking back to my experience, when Annette encountered me I was a proverbial open book. Open, fully exposed, fully vulnerable, and it didn't matter to me. I'm actually not certain it would have mattered even if I were in control. Something prevented me from caring about the implications of my behavior. It was like when I was in the car in the middle of the pond. I let go and let God, truly and fully. Perhaps at that moment I needed not to fear and something removed that possibility from my being. This may well be the power of the Holy Spirit.

When Laura was far from home, something forced her to leave the group and retreat to a quiet hotel room where she found Annette. At that point the very essence of her being was fully exposed and she was incapable of controlling herself. Perhaps for some of us the possibility of being in control needs to be removed to pierce through the veil of fear that holds our souls hostage. A definition of the word *hostage* includes a "person or group of people whose freedom of action is restricted or controlled by a more powerful organization by implied threats or other means." The "more powerful organization" may be evil, and the "other means" may be fear. Think about the word *fear*. Meditate on it. Don't you envision an imaginary barrier between you and the issue you need to address? What makes you fearful or anxiety-ridden? Envision your mind-body connection. Is it stilted? Is it contained? Fear impacts your body, mind, and spirit. That means it impacts your relationships, each and every one of them.

What about the role of fear in opening yourself up to God? Perhaps it doesn't prevent a direct relationship with Him, but it certainly prevents a full one. Do you openly praise God? Do you willingly spread the good news? Do you willingly act out the good news, or does some invisible hurdle keep your involvement in check? Do we fear being viewed as different from others? Do we fear being feared? What power we have! Those who fear us actually manifest the very struggle within our souls. Should we strive to be fully free, or just free enough to exist comfortably in society? *Perhaps fear kills souls.*

What about Tracy? Fear challenged her for most of her life. Why? Because she repeatedly experienced the effects of other peoples' fear when she exposed her true self to them. From a young age she restructured herself to fit within everyone else's "bell curve of normalcy." To what end? Who wins in that scenario? Perhaps the ugly faces and scary people that Tracy saw as a little girl were actually fear personified—fear of the truth, fear of judgment, fear of others, fear others have of the truth. Perhaps Tracy's early visitations were personifications of negative energy. Yes, energy. Fear is an energy and it is in our lives to prevent the soul's development.

When Laura and I spoke about the fear of exposing little bits of ourselves through these stories, the conversations merely skimmed the surface of real, deep-rooted fear. We knew we had to work through the layers of fear to see, much less touch, the truth. That led us to question why it is so hard to live fully in the truth. It's hard because we live in a society that creates and supports a thick layer of fear and does not readily offer the tools necessary to shovel through it. How does society do this? Distractions. Think about the material goods you have accumulated in your life. Now think about losing them. If you did not have as many things, the fear of losing something meaningful would less likely include something material. Individuals who live with fewer material goods seem to be better positioned for spiritual enlightenment. They may live closer to it.

We are beginning to realize the role fear plays in spirituality. Anything that prevents light and truth is evil and is equivalent to a perpetual total eclipse of the sun. Darkness that devours life-giving light suffocates our souls. We need to emerge from the darkness and bid it farewell, once and for all.

THE JOURNEY FORWARD: ANGELS IN THE CITY OF ANGELS

In the spring of 2010, God extended his reach to me and members of my family when my mother passed away. She and my dad lived in the same neighborhood outside of Los Angeles as my brother Jim, sister Marybeth, and their families. In the months leading to her death, my East Coast siblings and I flew across the country a lot. During our trips we witnessed the toll numerous health issues took on her body, ones that necessitated life-sustaining kidney dialysis beginning the year before. This being said, the six of us were shielded from the true nature of her suffering until shortly before her death.

During her decline, we readily acknowledged how lucky we were to have her. She and Dad had been married nearly fifty-three years. They had been blessed with six healthy children and fourteen healthy grandchildren. Our spouses and significant others were also privy to my mother's love. Unfortunately, not one of these facts made a dent in the grief we suffered when she died. It was deep, complicated, and immensely personal.

My mom's medical nightmare began earlier in the decade with a diagnosis of kidney cancer. She survived the cancer but suffered its consequences. She spent Christmas 2009 and the following three weeks in the hospital due to an extremely painful bout of diverticulitis. Emphysema, a by-product of forty-plus years of smoking, complicated her treatment. Less than two weeks before she died, she had emergency surgery to place stents in her heart and remove a significant portion of her colon. She was a fighter by all accounts and survived the surgeries, but her body ultimately could not defend against the relentless assaults it suffered.

With the exception of a week here or there, Mom was in the hospital from Christmas to the day she died. Every day without fail my dad and some member of the family saw her. They all were immersed in dedication. By early April my brother Jim was asked to honor her wishes to die at home, his home. She asked my father for permission to stop fighting for a life she wasn't able to live anymore.

The last time my brothers and I were summoned back to California, Jim somberly told us the devastating news that Mom was coming home to his house the next morning, and hospice would be with her until she passed. We struggled to comprehend his words as we were forced to adjust to the strange reality of waiting for a loved one to pass.

The next morning Jim took my dad to be with Mom while the rest of us waited at his house for the hospice workers. They planned to convert the guest room into a final resting place, complete with special bed and medical equipment. My sister worked that morning and planned to go directly to the house later that afternoon. Before noon my eldest brother arrived in California, and we began to divvy up tasks. Eager to fill the guest room with flowers and balloons, he left for the florist while the three of us remaining siblings ran errands. By early afternoon, we left for the hospital, too anxious to wait any longer for our mother to be transported to the house.

As my younger brother turned the car onto Sunset Boulevard toward the hospital, Jim called, frantic, and told us to "get here now." I immediately called my sister, and with numb and surreal anticipation, my siblings and I rushed to our mother's side.

My mother held on to life long enough for all of us to be with her. As I entered the hospital room, I was shocked to observe my mother in the process of dying. Her body and her very essence were shutting down before my eyes, systematically and permanently closing operations. My family was in a state of sustained shock. We knew we were unable to reverse the events we witnessed.

Time stands still for no one. Dad suggested we each whisper heartfelt sentiments into her ears, and we did so. He went last. It was evident her last breath was upon us. We each placed our hands on the parts of her body that were not bruised, transmitting nothing but pure love to her heart, her face, arms, legs, and shoulders. It was the most intimate and deeply spiritual moment of my life. As if on cue, her body hastened the process to enable her spirit to fly. We prayed over her, first the Our Father then the Hail Mary, as she peacefully passed away. She loved God and wanted to be with Him. He, in turn, was with us as her body expired to free her soul.

The days afterward were filled with preparations for Mom's funeral. Dad needed to make decisions but resisted doing so. He had lost the love of his life and his best friend; she was the woman God sent to join him in his journey through life. As we sadly attended our chores, we were blessed with several clear messages that Mom was with God, pain free and happy. They came by way of angels.

My sister volunteered to drive some of us to the wake. I immediately jumped in the front seat of her car and encouraged her young sons and our niece to join us. We planned to drive north on Sunset Boulevard to make our way to the Pacific Coast Highway. As she turned the corner from our brother's house onto Sunset, we were somber and spoke quietly in an effort to maintain a sense of calm. I noticed a gentleman standing by himself on the sidewalk in the middle of the block. He appeared to be a jolly, older man, dressed in a casual Key West-type shirt and a pair of khaki shorts. A cowboy hat hung low on his brow. As we approached, he lifted up his head, smiled, bowed, and tipped his hat to us. I recognized him instantly. He was our Uncle Jimmy, our mom's older brother who had died almost ten years earlier. I quickly turned to my sister. I couldn't believe my eyes!

"Did you see that man? It was Uncle Jimmy!"

"Oh my goodness; it was him!" She saw him too! Our college-aged niece strained to look back at the man. When she did, he was gone. Marybeth and I looked at one another quizzically and remained silent until we arrived at the funeral parlor.

"God must have sent Uncle Jimmy to let us know mom was pain free and with her family in heaven." Marybeth quivered as she spoke; she had such mixed emotions. For just a moment we were afforded comfort in the midst of grief.

THE JOURNEY FORWARD: ANGELS IN THE CITY OF ANGELS

Later that evening it dawned on me that the man we saw wasn't our Uncle Jimmy; God must have provided an apparition of someone my sister and I would immediately recognize. As we entered the church for Mom's funeral, I shared our experience with our dad. Numb, he listened but responded that he wished it was he who had received a sign. He wanted to be reassured she was free of the pain and suffering. I spoke with the pastor in a sincere and somewhat desperate attempt to affirm our experience. As I relayed the details about Uncle Jimmy, he nodded his head in agreement and confidently acknowledged God's glory.

Several days later, those of us who live on the East Coast needed to return home. I arranged to fly home with one brother and the girlfriend of another. Shortly after we boarded the plane we were delayed due to a bad storm. To pass the time, we struck up conversations with two women who sat closest to us. In between the silence, we casually joked about current events and such. The woman sitting across from me, the quieter of the two, asked what the three of us were doing in California. We grew somber.

"Our mom died. We are returning from her funeral." The woman expressed her condolences. "What was your mother's name again?" she asked. I found the question odd since she hadn't asked her name before.

"Joan," I politely answered. She raised her eyebrows.

"My name is Joan. And her last name?" I told her.

"My last name begins with *P* as well." She said as she looked directly at me. I was perplexed. My brother turned to the woman sitting closest to him. She was an older gal, quite bubbly and outspoken. He asked her name.

"Mary," she said. Mary was our grandmother's name. She had died just over two years before our mom. All five of us raised our eyebrows. I broke the tension.

"Clearly God has sent Joan and Mary to accompany us to make sure we get home safely." The women nodded their heads in agreement. I cannot describe the elation that comes from knowing God is with me. In that moment there was nothing to fear; there was only joy. We wished the women well and thanked them for their part in our journey.

Two days later I called Marybeth at work to see how she was doing. She is a marketing representative for a body products company and effortlessly handles customers in a warm and informative manner. She was incredibly close to my mother and suffered deeply from her passing. After some preliminary conversation, I listened to her relay the following story.

A prospective customer called the day before to gather information on certain body products. She was extremely pleasant, kind, and inquisitive. They spent near twenty minutes on the phone together. Marybeth realized she hadn't gotten the necessary contact information and apologized for not asking her name. Without hesitation the woman responded.

"Joan Theresa." My sister almost fell off of her seat. Joan Theresa is my mother's name.

I called my dad later to share these stories of blessed signs from heaven. He was silent on the phone and then began to sob.

"It's so wonderful you have the ability to believe these things. I am so happy for you, but I only wish your mother would send a message to *me*. I miss her so much."

I cried; my effort to comfort him resulted in extreme dismay. Not only was I sad for him, I was a bit upset with myself. Was I calloused to have shared these stories in such a hopeful and grateful manner? My father was alone for the first time in fifty-two years. Was I insensitive to his grief?

"I'm sorry, Dad, I didn't mean to upset you, but I'm afraid I have done just that."

He understood.

"You know, your mother was much more spiritual than me. I would go to church and all, but your mother would think about things and talk about her faith in a way I never could." It became clear to me that my dad was struggling with his own beliefs.

"Your mother had the chance to read the first two chapters of your book before she died." I was startled. I had sent the draft to my parents during one of my mother's hospital stays and attached a note to let me know what they thought. Secretly, I wanted my mother to read the draft and accept the invitation to peek into my soul. It was my desperate attempt to learn more about her. I was too fearful to ask her questions directly because she was such a private person, so I thought if I started the conversation by letting her read my thoughts, she might open up too. I was too late.

"Mom got to read the draft?" I asked, wanting to make sure I heard him correctly.

He said, "Yes, and she loved it."

"She did?" I asked.

"Yep, she loved every word of it."

My dad knew how important my mother's approval was to me, and I could tell how happy he was to relay such good news. As relieved as I was, I was devastated by my failure to release the fear that prevented me from pursuing conversations with her. Like Laura, I regretted the absence of deep, meaningful conversations with my mom. I yearned to sit and learn about her perspectives, her life decisions and fears, but mostly about the things that came between us. I wanted to clean up our relationship to enable a lasting connection between our souls before she died. I never took the chance, and I regret it.

"And you? Did you read it?" My father had taken lessons on writing children's books, a personal favorite of his. I figured his feedback would be more structural.

"Yes, I did. Honestly, it's very interesting and intimate, but I couldn't quite follow some of what you wrote. I guess I don't really think in those terms."

He was being completely honest, and I told him how much I appreciated his comments. As we continued to speak, I realized that while it was always easier for me to speak to my dad, it was my mom who really understood me.

We turned our conversation to the upcoming graduations of my nieces and nephews, his grandchildren. Before my mom died, she asked him to represent her at all family graduations, if possible. He struggled with the thought of leaving their home so soon after she passed, but he had given her his word. I encouraged him to push through his pain and sadness, and, yes, his fear of being alone, to honor her wishes. He did, and stayed with our family first.

While my dad was with us, we took walks, lots of walks. He missed walking. The months leading to my mother's death were so filled with medical issues and emergencies that my dad had given up on taking care of himself. To heal, he first had to rest; then he had to exercise. During one of our walks, he spoke honestly about his struggle.

"I always said I believed in heaven. I don't know what I believe anymore. I want heaven to be real, and I want to believe Mom is at peace and with God and her parents and sister and brother, but I don't know. I keep wondering whether I'm just fooling myself because the thought that she's not is too much to bear."

He cried while I stood next to him, helpless. I reminded him of the signs our family members received. He calmed himself and then shared the most wonderful news with me.

"I was packing to come here. I was in my bedroom and laying out my clothes to make sure I had everything. While I was packing, I was talking to Mom about not being ready to leave. I didn't want to leave California so soon, and I really didn't want to be alone. You know I always wanted her with me. Anyhow, while I was talking to her, on my right side, over my right shoulder, Mom spoke to me. She said, 'Frank, I'm right here.'"

He was inconsolable. As we hugged, I looked to heaven and thanked God.

The graduations were wonderful, proud moments. Dad dutifully made his rounds and represented my mother with love. Weeks passed. My sister was very depressed and missed our mother terribly. In one of our telephone conversations she lamented her daily drive to work; the route she took passed the dialysis center, doctors' offices, and hospital our mother was required to frequent. On her way to work that morning she was preoccupied with her own spiritual beliefs. She said she was distressed and worried that our mom wasn't really pain free. She had cried so hard she had to pull the car over as she drove up Sunset Boulevard. As she did, she looked over to the sidewalk and saw Uncle Jimmy once again. He looked at her, tipped his hat, and then smiled. She bawled as she clutched her chest in thanks and relief and then gathered herself enough to continue the commute into work.

She hadn't seen Uncle Jimmy since the day of the wake, and she hasn't seen him since.

Perhaps God uses human likenesses to send me and my family messages because we need unequivocal signs that He is with us, that He hears our pleas. Perhaps we are not adept at construing less obvious messages. Families such as Laura's are.

MOM'S DIMES

Last summer, Laura's daughter Morgan attended a two-week college-level class in fashion merchandising. Her decision to live on campus as a high school summer student was more complicated than the simple writing of a check; it would be the first time Morgan spent an extended period away from home. While her desire to attend the program trumped her fear of the unknown, she readily confessed her concern about how it all would work out. Because she spoke freely to her mother, anticipation and anxiety filled the days leading to her departure. Laura prayed to God for his help. More than anything, she wanted her daughter to have the confidence and assistance necessary for success in the program. She asked God to help Morgan overcome the anxiety with which she struggled for years.

Underneath the calm, loving assurances she gave her daughter, Laura was terrified. She wouldn't be available to help her daughter overcome a potentially distressing situation. But Morgan knew the complexities of her decision and told her mother she was ready to confront her anxieties head on; she was determined to integrate seamlessly into a college setting.

The summer program began with campus staff eager to begin the two-week session. After a tour of the college and attention to some administrative details, Laura, Curt, and Carsen were encouraged to say their goodbyes to Morgan before she was swiftly whisked away. Laura helplessly watched Morgan struggle to keep herself from becoming too overwhelmed. Before she could reassure her once more, a young school guide directed the students into a campus building. With nothing left to do or say, the family turned toward the parking lot. Laura walked to the car filled with concern for her daughter.

On the way home, they stopped for lunch. Their conversation revolved around Morgan and how wonderful the experience was going to be for her. As they left the restaurant, Curt bent down and casually picked up a dime he saw lying on the ground. He handed the dime to Carsen. This caused Laura to smile. Dimes always seemed to appear at the oddest moments, typically after she would pray to her mom for help with something. Laura tucked the incident away into her memory.

Curt said he needed to run an errand, so Laura and Carsen waited in the front of the home supply store while he shopped. Carsen looked down on the aisle floor and said, "Mom, look, another dime!" Now Laura couldn't contain herself. She became emotional. It was no coincidence, at least not to Laura, that reassurances came by way of dimes. Taking the dimes as a sign from God, Laura knew Morgan would be alright.

When the family returned home, Tracy called to see how Morgan made out. Laura told her the stories of the dimes from earlier in the day. Tracy laughed.

"Oh that was just Mommy, and she wanted to let you know everything is okay and Morgan will be just fine. Mom sends me dimes too!"

Laura stared at the phone. Tracy never mentioned the meaning of dimes before!

"Why in the world do we humans keep these stories to ourselves?"

It was a message that could have been ignored. Instead, Laura thought enough to speak to her sister about the phenomena and learned of a connection that otherwise would have remained hidden.

Perhaps Laura's sensitivities to signs and symbols make her more open to receiving messages through them. After all, she is artistic and easily drawn to shapes like spirals and circles. Perhaps her mother is best able to communicate with her by using dimes because they are circular. Laura interprets their presence as reassurance of God's grace and of her part in something much bigger than any given moment in which she finds herself.

GRACE IN MOTION: THE ONENESS IN OUR JOURNEYS

For Tracy, dreams and visions seem to be God's preferred method of communication. During these times, she is at peace and devoid of fear and, being so, receives God's messages without the static of everyday life. When asked about her vision of God healing Dave, the one we discussed early in the book, she remains humble. While she knows she witnessed something miraculous, she likewise knows God would never have let her see anything unintended. Perhaps that vision was intended as a small glimpse into her own soul. Lucky her! And when she was lost and questioned the purpose of her amazing gifts, God sent Ann to relay a direct and divine message of reassurance to her.

For Laura and I, while we viewed our Annettes as angels, we remained curious as to whether there was something more than coincidence to connect the names of these women. For purposes of our investigation, we treated Tracy's Ann as equivalent to our Annettes. We opened our Bibles and explored the Internet to find out whether the names represented specific puzzle pieces to assist us in our spiritual journeys. They did.

The name Annette comes from the Hebrew 'Hannah', meaning grace. Grace is described as "divine, unmerited favor from God," and "an enabling power sufficient for progression." Need I write more? The discovery was monumental. The definitions lingered in our thoughts as Laura and I stared at one another in disbelief. In one brief moment, we shared unique joy, true enlightenment, and a glimpse into each other's soul. It was a true "aha" moment. These women were grace personified.

Earlier in our lives we willingly released ourselves to God and He responded. Years later, He responded again by giving us the puzzle pieces necessary to propel our spiritual journeys forward.

God's grace isn't intended just for a select few. Curiosities present themselves everyday, it's just that some of us are so numbed to the obvious we dismiss them as coincidence. God is all around us. He is constantly reaching out to us, seeking to draw us ever closer to Him. With the gift of free will we are as close to Him as our hearts and minds permit us to be.

Through our stories we hope to have illuminated the river of souls at our disposal. Tracy's and Laura's mother died many years ago, yet her soul remains available to her family. My mother died more recently, yet her soul quickly sought the opportunity to soothe and comfort my family members. We believe their souls continue to do God's work. We believe God hears all prayers for reassurance, strength, and guidance and he answers each in the manner best suited for the recipient.

Clearly God is with us. To help Him help us, we must see what we are looking at and listen to what we hear. It is an attainable goal. All we need is the willingness to open our hearts, quiet our minds, and to think.

PLEASE JOIN US ON THE JOURNEY

We hope to have paved the way for those of you who struggle to incorporate otherwise unexplainable occurrences into your daily lives. Tracy's life is an extraordinary example of spiritual existence; Laura's, a celebration of spiritual beliefs. Mine too. Throughout the book-writing process, the three of us invested the time to learn about one another. We were rewarded with 'puzzle pieces' that demonstrated how all lives can intertwine on an amazing journey towards God. And despite being far from perfect, through God's many graces we have been afforded endless opportunities for enlightenment. Our journeys are far from over. We remain humbled by the power of the Holy Spirit and yearn for future "Annette" moments to help soothe and support our souls. We do our best and hope you join us here on the pathway to God.

ABOUT THE AUTHORS

Cheryl McCausland and Laura Terry have been friends for over twenty years. Cheryl lives in New York with her husband and three children. She has been an attorney since 1987 and is active in the community. She teaches religion and leads a youth group at her church. Laura lives in New Jersey with her husband, two daughters, and loyal dog, Luke. Upon graduation from college, Laura worked in the computer technology field. After the birth of her second child, she began her career as an interior decorator. She volunteers at her local church.

ENDNOTES

[1] Deepak Chopra, *Why Is God Laughing? The Path to Joy and Spiritual Optimism*, New York: Harmony Books, 2008, p.181

[2] Rod Termperton (c) 1982 Rodsongs (PRS) Administered by Almo Music Corp. in the U.S. and Canada; In the remaining territories by Rondor Music (London) Ltd (PRS)

[3] Deepak Chopra, *Why Is God Laughing? The Path to Joy and Spiritual Optimism*, New York: Harmony Books, 2008, p.172-173

Made in the USA
Charleston, SC
16 March 2012